do
your
scroggin

don't forget your scroggin

A HOW-TO HANDBOOK FOR NEW ZEALAND TRAMPING

Sarah Bennett & Lee Slater

craig potton publishing

First published in 2007 by Craig Potton Publishing

Craig Potton Publishing
98 Vickerman Street, PO Box 555,
Nelson, New Zealand
www.craigpotton.co.nz

ISBN 978-1-877333-71-2

Printed by Astra Print Ltd, Wellington

Contents

scroggin. *Tramping*. Also **scrogen**, and occas. abbrev. scrog (see quot. 1971). [Origin uncertain: poss. f. *scr*(an + h)*og* (*in*).] A mixture of dried fruits, nuts, chocolate, etc., eaten by trampers as a high energy snack. Also *attrib*.

1940 *Tararua Tramper* Mar. 7 We had our breakfast of 'scroggin'. **1948** MOIRS *Guide Book* (2nd edn.) 88 The best quality of raisins, dates, nuts, etc., should be selected to make up a 'scroggin' mixture to nibble when stopping for a spell. **1950** *Canterbury Mountaineer* 45 The 'Scroggin Bag' was produced with heavy demands on chocolate etc. **1958** *Tararua* Sept. 26 If any word originating in the mountain clubs deserves to be incorporated in the language it is perhaps *scroggin*. That mixture of raisins, sultanas, chocolate, nuts, boiled lollies, a mixture of bits and pieces of whatever one fancies, was evolved to fill the need for a sustaining, palatable, easily-carried food, one as readily available for a bite snatched in a cold, wet, momentary halt as for a welcome spell in the warmth and sun. The word seems to come from Otago but its derivation is not clear. **1971** ARMFELT *Catching Up* 137 'I brought some scrog, and a thermos of hot coffee.' He...handed him the mixture of raisins, nuts and squares of dark chocolate. **1971** *Listener* 19 Apr. 56 It was hard yakka, nothing but a plate of burgoo and a handful of scroggin since sparrow-chirp. **1980** *NZ Woman's Weekly* 7 Jan. 83 Scrogen: 1 cup peanuts, 3/4 cup dried apricots, 1 135 gram block energy chocolate, 1/2 cup mixed dried fruit, 1/4 cup sunflower seeds, 1/2 cup coconut, 2 tablespoons powered glucose. Roast the peanuts at 180° C for 10–15 minutes, or until lightly golden. Cool. Chop the apricots and chocolate coarsely. In a strong plastic bag, put the peanuts, apricots, chocolate, mixed fruit, sunflower seeds, coconut and glucose. Shake to combine. Secure closed. Use as a high energy snack food. **1991** *Dominion* (Wellington) 9 Mar. 10 'Scroggin? What the hell's scroggin?' Scroggin, I can tell you, is the tramper's friend—an energy-sustaining mixture of peanuts, chocolate and raisins.

The Oxford Dictionary of New Zealand English

Really it would be worth the trudge ... to visit this spur on a calm moonlight night, when surely the fairies would provide us with unimagined joys and visions of loveliness.

You gaze in wonder, become contemplative, and suddenly feel very small and insignificant. You get for once, at any rate, the correct perspective, and discover that your ambitions, petty successes, and yourself, are merely pinpoints in immensity. The mountains have a corrective power on mental perspective which compels inward acknowledgement.

Frank Penn,
from *Across the Tararuas*, 1920

Why go tramping?

Well, why would you? It's all blisters, bad food and sleepless nights in a leaky tent, isn't it? Trust us: it most certainly is not. Walking is the most popular active leisure pursuit in New Zealand, and tramping is just walking with boots on.

We are trampers and we love it. Lots of our friends do too. There are as many reasons to tramp as places to do it, and here are only a few:

- **Discover** New Zealand's great outdoors. Some of the most beautiful scenery in the world is on your doorstep. However, to see the best bits, you need to venture beyond the road-end, through the gate, and quite often up the hill.
- **Get fit** and **stay fit**. Whilst taking in those breathtaking views, you'll be doing yourself a favour too – walking is the best exercise you can get.
- **Learn** about New Zealand's rich natural and human history. Incredible tales abound; every place has its own amazing story to tell.
- **Develop new skills**: navigation, outdoor survival, first aid, camp cookery, conservation, even meteorology and astronomy. The more you tramp, the smarter you'll be.
- **Meet new people** and **make new friends**, both weird and wonderful, from all walks of life and many corners of the world. Friendships forged on the track often stand up well to the test of time.

- **Unwind and relax.** Trudging uphill with a big fat pack on your back ... how relaxing can that be? Okay, we'll admit it: it's sometimes pretty hard work, but it's still a holiday for the mind. Escape the trappings of modern life. Get back to nature. Enjoy some peace and quiet.

Sounds pretty good, doesn't it? By now you'll be wanting to lace those boots up and get out there. That's what we want you to do. But before you go, we've got some tips and tricks to help you on your way.

Tramping isn't always easy but it should be enjoyable and rewarding. If you're not having fun, maybe you're not doing it right?

Whether you're new to tramping or just unfamiliar with the New Zealand experience, this book is for you. It offers all the most important things we've learnt so far, combined with a heap of advice from other trampers of all ages and levels of experience. We'll show you how to get out on the track, what to do once you get there, and help you discover your own answer to the question, *why go tramping?*

We expect you'll get fully hooked, so please write and tell us about it. We welcome any feedback on this book – and your own tramping stories. Write to us at PO Box 24-103, Wellington. We'll be glad to hear from you.

Clothing and footwear

The purpose of tramping clothing is to protect you from the elements and regulate body temperature. Wearing optimal clothing will make your tramp safer, more comfortable and easier. The ideal outfit will vary with each tramp and the time of year, but the bottom line is: **always be prepared for the *worst* conditions.**

Fortunately, we live in an age of high-tech fabrics and a highly competitive outdoor apparel market. A visit to your tramping outfitter will reveal a stupendous array of clothing with its fancy branding and technological specifications. Don't feel overwhelmed. If you strip away the frippery, you'll see that the principles are the same: **the goal is comfortable, functional clothing that is durable, lightweight and quick-drying.** And it needs to fit right. You'll soon wear things in and work out what fits best alongside other garments. A well-selected walking wardrobe offers absolute comfort. The fact that much of it is super-stylish is a bonus.

There are some general rules when it comes to kitting yourself out, and the first one is: **do your research**. Ask around your friends and fellow trampers – what are they wearing and why? **Shop around**: really good tramping retailers will know their stuff. Good ones are likely to be independent (not part of a chain), specialising in outdoor gear while offering a wide range of brands. Their staff will be keen users of their own products – if you suspect they're not, go elsewhere. Tell them what you think you need, and listen to their recommendations. Ask about their most popular brands, and seek explanations on quality versus price. Look closely at the workmanship. **Try before you buy.** And while we thoroughly recommend pursuing end-of-season sales (there's a glut of this stuff and bargains aplenty), **don't scrimp** on your clothing. Your personal comfort is of paramount importance.

The walking wardrobe

The secret to practicality and comfort is **layering** – longjohns under trousers under overpants; undergarments under midlayer under shell. Add and subtract as you start to get hot, cold or wet.

The advantage of a layered clothing system is that you can – with practice – **take clothes for every eventuality** while keeping their total weight reasonably low. Over-packing is common, especially when you're new to tramping, but this is a self-correcting error. When it's time to pick up the pack and swing it on your back, you might have second thoughts about those heavy jeans (... don't even think about it!). And allow us to state the obvious here: **it's better to be too warm than not warm enough.**

You'll need to **wear pretty much the same outfit every day.** For most of us – used to changing clothes daily and sometimes more than once – this might seem a little unseemly. But in an era of lemon-scented squeakiness you might actually find it surprisingly liberating. Don't get us wrong: clean, dry underwear is a must, but a bit of dirt in the outerlayers isn't going to kill you. You'll soon become adept at ranking your socks on the dirtometer and washing your undies on the hop.

You must **carry clothes in reserve**, especially socks and undergarments, and you should always have something dry and warm to change into at the end of the day. You may well be sleeping in it.

But it's not bedtime yet. As with any tramp, let's start feet first ...

> You'll find a comprehensive **clothing checklist** at the back of this book.

Boots

A good pair of boots is one of the most important purchases you will make – an investment in your tramping future. You'll really be putting them through their paces: slick tree roots and slippery mud; big fat boulders and sharp scree; rope ladders, three-wire bridges and fast-flowing rivers. Tramping boots protect your precious feet in a way that sneakers or even walking shoes can't: giving you grip, taking the knocks and supporting the ankles.

There are barrack-loads of boots about, so brace yourself for some serious legwork. Set out with comfort as your priority: they must fit perfectly. Also, avoid being swayed by bargains: **buy the best and most comfortable pair you can afford**. If well-cared for they may last more than 10 years, so they'll easily earn their keep.

Tramping boots come in many makes and models, from lightweight synthetics (for short day hikes on easy terrain) through to heavy, stiff-soled alpine boots (designed for rocks, snow and ice, and able to take crampons). The upper will be either full-grain leather, Nubuck leather or Cordura. Leather is generally regarded as superior, being tough, hardwearing, waterproof and offering maximum support and insulation. They are also the more expensive option. Cordura boots – usually trimmed with leather – aren't quite as robust or waterproof, although they can be sprayed with special treatments to retain maximum water resistance. They are, however, lighter, more breathable and faster drying.

Pay careful attention to the sole of the boot. There should be a clearly defined heel and a 'knobbly' tread fashioned out of high quality rubber (our first choice is Vibram, available on many boot brands worldwide). These features are essential for keeping your grip in New Zealand conditions: wet, slippery and tricky under foot.

Have a think about the sort of boot you need *before* you bowl into the shop. Will you be a fair-weather day-tripper or a gnarly overnighter? How far will you go, over what terrain, and how heavy will your pack be? Now you're ready to shop.

TIPS FOR FITTING BOOTS

The best person to help you choose your boots is your retailer. They should know their stock inside out and be expert at helping you fit them. A troublesome boot at the outset will seldom come good, so put your best foot forward and try some on:

- Try before you buy – every pair in town (and beyond) if needs be.
- Wear thick wool socks – you will be when you're walking.
- When you first don the boot, push your foot to the front: there should be about a finger-width of room at the back of the heel. This is a rough indication that the boot is the right size.
- Take the time (every time) to line up the tongue and lace them up right. The boot should fit snugly around the ankle and instep; movement here will cause blisters. But there should be a bit of room across the forefoot and toes. Your toes should have sufficient wiggle-room, and the big toe shouldn't be hard up against the end. Cramped toes downhill will surely ruin a grand day out.
- Wear them around the shop. Around and around, up and down. They may be stiff, but pay attention to any potentially troublesome pressure points.

It's unwise to embark on an epic trip in your brand new boots. **Break them in** over short trips or walks around the block. For tips on avoiding blisters, see page 66.

Look after your boots and they will reward you with loyal service. On the trail, resist the temptation to dry sodden boots in front of a raging fire – they'll become tough as old boots. Better to **dry them gently**, if you can. And come morning, donning a damp boot is nothing to be bothered by. A warm woolly sock will soon see your toes toasty.

At the end of your trip, **clean your boots well** with warm water and a soft brush. Stuffing them with crumpled newspaper will speed up drying of the inner. Once dry, **nourish and protect them** with appropriate conditioner. Leather boots should be treated with a wax or dubbin, while Cordura boots should be sprayed with a recommended product – your retailer will tell you what's best. Store your boots clean and dry, so when you drag them out next spring they'll be shipshape, supple and water repellent.

Other footwear

For short trips over easy terrain, a **walking shoe** will probably do for you. Not to be confused with a sneaker, cross-trainer or suchlike, these are made especially for off-road walking trips, identifiable by features such as a heavy-duty upper (often leather, Nubuck or tough synthetic), a thick rubber sole with deep tread and a moulded insole that affords plenty of support.

Some manufacturers also make a **walking sandal**. These offer the benefits of being relatively lightweight and airy; indeed, they are often very comfortable and therefore perfectly acceptable, but only for short, easy summer walks.

For overnight trips, you'll need another shoe to wear in the hut or around camp. Plastic clogs are popular and practical, but super-light sneakers, sandals or jandals are also good. Don't be afraid to wear sandals or jandals with socks. Chances are, way out here in the wilderness, you won't bump into anyone you know.

MY FIRST PAIR OF tramping boots was a cheap pair of leather boots I'd bought for farm work when I was a high school student. The boots lasted okay for the first few weekend trips, and so I embarked on my first week-long trip with some friends in the Kaweka Ranges. The trip saw us crossing and recrossing the Mangatainoka River as we worked our way up the valley. During one particularly bouldery crossing I complained, 'I can feel every stone through these damn boots.'

When we reached the far bank, I discovered there was a very good reason for that – the whole sole had somehow ripped off in the river, and was by now well on its way to Hawke's Bay. I was left with a boot on one foot, but something resembling a badly made moccasin on the other. Still four days tramping to go. The moccasin disintegrated after a further two days. However hardwearing they are, I don't recommend tramping in just a Norsewear sock.

Shaun Barnett, in 'Some huts do have 'em', *Wilderness*, May 2000

Undergarments

The layer next to your skin should be chosen carefully, because it has to deal with sweat. In warm conditions, a little bit of moisture next to the skin is fine, but in cool conditions **sweat can dramatically affect your ability to keep warm.** Different fabrics deal with moisture differently. While you might have a few suitable garments in your wardrobe already, be prepared to invest in some extras.

The ideal undergarment – whether longjohns, singlet or t-shirt – will not trap moisture next to the skin. The best fabrics for the job are made out of **merino** wool, **polypropylene, polyester,** or **merino–synthetic** mix – *not* cotton. Some people swear by silk because it's lightweight and comfortable, but it won't be as durable as other options.

Merino (see overleaf), now finely woven for comfort, will absorb sweat but still keep you warm. However, it is reasonably expensive and takes much longer to dry.

The **synthetics** (i.e. all but merino and other woollens) are hydrophobic, that is: they hate water. These fabrics effectively wick moisture away from your body, rather than trapping it next to your skin where it causes evaporative heat loss – that's what cotton will do. Lightweight and breathable, hydrophobic fabrics are excellent at helping regulate your body temperature. Polypropylene is the cheaper option, but has the disadvantage of retaining odour; polyester is softer and less smelly.

On hot days, lightweight **cotton** singlets and t-shirts are fine. Cotton traps sweat, but this will quickly evaporate, leaving you pleasantly cooled. But if there's a nip in the air, brace yourself. That damp t-shirt will turn cold and clammy. You have been warned!

When the sun shines, it's tempting to strip down to your singlet while a refreshing breeze distracts you from its intensity. But remember: our sun causes nasty sunburn and serious long-term damage. Consider a light, long-sleeve cotton or polyester shirt – they are very effective at keeping you cool while affording all-day sun protection. Avoid the constant slather of ikky sunblock. Avoid the unsightly t-shirt tan. Avoid turning into an old leather handbag.

Midlayers and outerwear

From the underwear outwards it's a matter of layering close-fitting garments according to the conditions.

For your top half, over your undergarments, we recommend more merino – simple long-sleeve tops or, in cooler conditions, the classic **zip-up turtleneck**. Consider the cuffs: thumb-loops are excellent at excluding a cold draught. Various manufacturers offer lots of other features such as chafe-avoiding seams and ventilation panels. The result is some fabulously functional and comfy garments – they aren't cheap, but they work hard and they last.

MIGHTY MERINO

Back in the 1970s and '80s, the scratchy woollen 'bush shirt' was the quintessential symbol of tramping in New Zealand. Wool has, in fact, long been the choice of the good keen Kiwi, offering vital warmth when wet, while being readily available and inexpensive. In recent years, local innovation and leaps in fabric technology have propelled one particular sheep into the global arena: merino. She's a very special sheep, for sure, and we've been flocking to her fleece in droves.

Merino is super-fine, premium quality wool, often woven or layered with synthetics to enhance functionality: polyester for lightweight warmth, nylon for durability, and Lycra for stretch. Merino mixes, often branded with fancy names such as Interfleece and Underfluff (... okay, we made those up), are incredibly popular – for good reason. Not only do these garments offer excellent insulation and breathability, they offer a high UV protection factor (30+) and are more fire resistant than synthetics. Merino is also stain resistant, machine washable and won't retain odours. They can get a bit pricey, but you'll usually get a good run out of them so they're actually quite a baaaaa-gain.

This lasagne of layers should be topped off with a **thick jumper** or **fleece jacket**, your essential insulation against the cold. Pure wool, while warm, offers little wind resistance – so you'll need a jacket over the top. Polyester fleece jackets really come into their own here, offering plenty of warmth while remaining lightweight (half the weight of wool) and quick-drying. Unfortunately though, many of these aren't particularly wind resistant either. Better still is the **soft-shell**, a jacket offering both a snug fleecy inner and a highly windproof outer. Some also offer a reasonable degree of water resistance, but not enough to leave your raincoat at home. Whichever you choose, look for features such as a zip-up front and a turtleneck.

Down jackets, worn at camp but not on the track, are the ultimate in warmth. Relatively light and compact, these keep you toasty warm on chilly evenings. You can sleep in a jacket too, allowing you to get away with a lighter sleeping bag; or stuff it into a sac and use it as a pillow.

Now, let's turn to your bottom, if we may. The traditional tramping attire is a pair of **shorts**, these days fashioned out of nylon and sporting fancy features such as an 'action gusset', but any pair of lightweight, comfortable shorts will do. Shorts offer the benefit of allowing a free range of movement, while being light and cool. A classic Kiwi tramping combo is shorts over longjohns, which offers extra warmth as well as protection from the sun/bugs/scratches (covering up is *by far* your best protection from sunburn and insect bites).

Some folk prefer **trousers**, despite the fact that they are prone to become wet and flappy. Avoid this by buying trousers with zip-off legs. These are a marvellous invention: zip them off to show off your shapely calves, or for extra ventilation, river crossings, muddy bog hops, etc. When the sun beats down or the sandflies attack, zip those legs back on and keep danger at bay.

In cold, wet and windy conditions, you'll need **overtrousers**. An acceptable option is the relatively cheap and unflattering parka-pants, pulled on over the top of your longjohns, shorts or trousers. Alternatively, you can buy fancier trousers made from Gore-Tex and the like. Midsummer sea-level trampers can probably leave these at home – a little rain is rather refreshing on the skin. But in alpine environments or on any trip where the conditions could turn cold, they are an essential part of your kit.

Jackets

A dependable waterproof jacket is a mainstay of your tramping gear and buying the right one will probably require as much effort as buying your boots. There are heaps of brands and styles on the market, so you'll have to do your research; most of the best are expensive. However, getting caught without a proper jacket is not only uncomfortable but dangerous, because this is the layer that will keep you warm *and* dry – at least, in theory. No jacket on the planet will keep you totally dry if you're battling through driving rain and sweating at the same time, but you'll be a lot better off with one than without.

A tramping jacket is unpadded, hooded, either hip-length or to the top of the thigh. The shorter jacket allows greater movement, and weighs a little less. Thigh-length, however, offers the benefits of a dry bottom: cascades of run-off will bypass your ass, and you won't get any soak-up when sitting on mossy logs. We therefore recommend the longer jacket. Look for a size roomy enough to cover all your layers comfortably – you should be able to move freely and easily. But don't buy too big: a loose fit will flap about and allow warm air to escape, and it weighs more of course.

There are many jackets on the market, and the selection process comes down mostly to a matter of materials: they all offer different benefits. Some things to consider:

- **Water resistance** – will it stand up to a downpour or just a light shower?
- **Breathability** – your active body will generate heat and sweat. Can it escape or will you get hot and clammy?
- **Durability** – will the fabric and construction stand up to high wear and repeated bush-bashing?
- **Style and fit** – is it the right length, does it have useful features such as pockets, drawstring hood, chafe-free seams, or adjustable cuffs? Is it comfortable?

- **Weight** – whether on your back or in your pack, does the weight justify the benefit?
- **Compactability** – how much precious room will it take up in your pack?
- **Cost** – as always, we recommend spending whatever is necessary, but maybe there's an acceptable compromise?

Waterproofing and breathability are your foremost considerations, and unless you've been living in a cave, you will know that **Gore-Tex** is the market leader, although many similar fabrics are now made.

These high-tech fabrics have a membrane which allows tiny body vapour droplets to escape to the surface while preventing larger rain- or snow-drops getting in. If this sounds too good to be true, then you're more than a little bit right: it won't work perfectly every time. These fabrics work best when you are hot and the outside temperature is cold. On a warm and wet day, you may find yourself sweaty regardless.

Gore-Tex and its friends come in different grades, so now let's talk about trade-offs. The heavier versions are more durable, an important factor when bush-bashing and dealing with abrasive pack straps; but of course they weigh more. The lighter versions ... well, you get the drift. Talk to your retailer or friends who are already wearing them. Think about the conditions you are likely to encounter in your tramping escapades.

Care for your (expensive) jacket by following the manufacturer's instructions. This usually involves gentle washing with natural soap (avoid detergent) and thorough drying away from sunlight. If the fabric starts to 'wet out' (i.e. drops stop beading on the surface), you'll need to re-treat it with a recommended product, and you *could* consider putting it through the dryer or ironing it (but check the instructions first).

Socks, hats and gloves

Buy proper tramping **socks**: that's good quality thick wool or wool –synthetic blends (no cotton please!). Most have extra padding around the toes and the heels. To cushion your feet and help prevent blisters, consider wearing a thinner pair or sock liner underneath. But watch for wrinkles, and don't let your feet get too squashed.

A **warm hat** is a must, all year round. Did you know, up to 70 per cent of your body heat can be lost through your head and neck? Even in high summer, the temperature can drop rapidly at night – especially in the mountains – and a long day's walk can leave you feeling a bit chilly. If you're tramping in especially cold conditions, consider taking two: donning a dry hat in the evenings is cheap, light insurance against the chill. Wool can be itchy so look for a fine blend or something fleecy.

Always take a **wide-brimmed hat** or **cap**. Depending on the terrain, you might be exposed to the cruel New Zealand sun all day long, and in summer even 10 minutes' exposure can be too much. Overcast and winter days are no exception: you can still get lightly toasted. A sunburnt face is painful and avoidable. Sunscreen alone is not enough. Slap on a hat.

Gloves complete your standard kit and should be packed at all times other than high-temperature trips. A cheap and generally adequate option is a pair of polypropylene gloves – but these aren't waterproof and won't do the job in very cold and wet conditions. There are plenty of other options, including a thin micro-fleece (also not waterproof) or a waterproof shell glove with a fleece liner: your best bet for colder conditions.

Optional extras

Any attempt at keeping your socks dry will be aided by a pair of **puttees** or **gaiters**. These are little overcoats that wrap around your lower leg, covering the top of your boot (puttees are anklets; gaiters cover the calf too). Their principal role is to fend off snow, ice, rain, dew and lashings of gluggy mud, but they'll also prevent stones and twigs from invading your boots, and bidibids and hookgrass infesting your socks. They also offer a bit of extra warmth, particularly if you're wearing shorts: only your knobbly knees will be exposed to the elements. Look for gaiters with cord or wire to secure them to your boots.

A pair of **sunglasses** are handy for bright days, and essential for snowy conditions.

The ubiquitous cotton **bandana** should always find its way into your pocket or pack. It has so many uses besides making you look like Willie Nelson. Wrap it around your neck to fend off the sun. Wear it Rambo-style to prevent sweat stinging your eyes. Blot the sweat from your brow and blow your nose. Dip it in a cooling stream and pat yourself deliciously down.

You'll find a comprehensive **clothing checklist** at the back of this book.

Equipment

We trampers and campers just love to talk equipment, an inexhaustible topic for conversation. There's so much stuff on the market: clever and compact, snazzy and stylish, and suddenly all *so* essential. Fortunately there's ample opportunity for new acquisitions and upgrades, whether you're branching out into different terrain or the old thingy just wore out. Gearing up is an endless quest for the lightest and best, and a very enjoyable quest it is too (even if it is rather expensive – but think of the money you save by going bush instead of flying to a tropical island to drink fancy cocktails).

Whether buying a tent or a torch, **do your homework**. Good gear costs good money, so aim to **buy right the first time**. Your outdoor retailer ought to prove invaluable in this mission: earthy, rugged types usually work in these shops because they love the outdoors. They've used the gear and they know it inside out; if you have any doubt whether they do, move on. Another good port of call is the monthly *Wilderness* magazine. Not only does it have product reviews in every issue, but it also produces an annual 'gear guide' with fairly wide coverage of market offerings. Ask your tramping friends for advice, too. Sound recommendations will avoid all manner of mistakes, including financial.

You'll find a comprehensive **equipment checklist** at the back of this book.

Good gear does go on sale, but only from time to time, and usually only slightly discounted. Bad gear, however, is always a bargain. Quality and price are closely correlated. If you want to be as well prepared and as comfortable as possible, **pay whatever it takes.**

Packs

At the risk of sounding like a broken record, we recommend you buy the best pack you can possibly afford. For overnight tramping, you'll need a pack with a **capacity** of 65–80 litres. For a short trip (1–2 nights) you may find 45–60 litres sufficient. For more ambitious types, packs run up to 95 litres, but you'd definitely struggle to carry it full to the brim. Also, many models feature an extendable lid, affording more space. Be sure to look for a *tramping* pack, not a *travel* pack: their harnesses and weight distributions differ, an important factor when walking all day. A full pack can weigh well over 20 kilos, but, Dear Reader, we advise you stick to around 16–20 kilos (men) and 14–18 kilos (women) for a 3–5 day tramp. See page 27 for tips on packing light.

Most manufacturers make their packs in different sizes, gauged on the length of your back. They are made from either **canvas or synthetic** material. Traditionally, New Zealand trampers favour canvas, which is reasonably waterproof and very hardwearing. Packs made from synthetic materials are considerably lighter and increasingly popular as more overseas brands come on to the market. Be warned though, some are more prone to wear and tear; others may afford less water resistance, particularly after a few years' use.

It's the **harness** that largely dictates comfort, load-bearing limits and price. The degree of adjustability varies greatly and is very important. As always, make comfort your priority. Look closely at the lumbar pad, hip belt and shoulder straps: you need quality padding to ensure perfect fit and optimum weight transfer. Some manufacturers make harnesses especially for women, with special contours and padding – well worth asking for. Bear in mind there's a trade off here: some fancy harnesses are heavy – they can differ by as much as a kilo, and that's before you've even packed anything. You might be better off with a simpler harness and a spare kilo up your sleeve.

Beyond the materials and harness, consider the **compartments, pockets** and **straps**. Do you want a separate base compartment, or an all-in-one? Do you need a zip-off daypack or a lid that converts to a bumbag? Is the lid extendable to give you extra capacity? Look at the pockets, inside and out: are they useful and in the right place? Are there good compression straps for battening everything down? Are there sufficient straps and loops for any extras? It's worth questioning whether you need all these bells and whistles. Every pocket, zip and strap has potential for leakage or breakage – and adds a little more weight. As a minimum, we recommend an easy-entry top pocket, preferably accessible from the rear (i.e. the side closest to your neck). That way, when you stop to rest and lay your pack down, you easily get to your scroggin or sunscreen.

There are many permutations, so **try before you buy**. Ask your retailer about the different makes and models. Get them to fit the pack and fill it with a decent load. It should fit snug against your back. The hip belt should sit on the hips (not on the waist), transferring much of the weight to the hips, and off the shoulders. The shoulder straps should fit snug over your shoulders; the sternum strap should be adjusted to ease the position of the shoulder straps and add a little bit of extra stability to the top half. **A well-fitting pack will allow you freedom to move**, without swinging from side to side. Be prepared to make minor adjustments as you go: a slight tweak of a strap can make all the difference.

You'll be amazed how much you can carry and how far you can walk with a comfortable pack. Conversely, a bad pack can make every step a real drag. Back and shoulder aches, pinches, pressure points and chafing will turn your tramp into an endurance test.

TOP TIPS FOR PACKING LIGHT AND RIGHT

Let's start with the bad news: you *will* encounter rain. And because it is absolutely imperative that you keep the contents of your pack dry (and no pack, no matter how fancy, is fully waterproof), the first thing you must do before you pack is buy a large, thick plastic **pack liner** from the DOC visitor centre or tramping shop. This goes *inside* your pack; those elasticated, fabric pack covers will not do the trick. Folk with a double-compartment pack will have to line both compartments.

The good news is we can help you lose weight. Trampers are obsessed with pack weight for very good reason. A heavy pack is not only energy sapping but potentially dangerous too – all that weight will alter your centre of gravity and those tricky ups and downs will become all the more hazardous. The general rule is that you shouldn't carry more than about 25 per cent of your body weight, although fit, strapping lads will bump that figure up to 30 per cent or even more.

So, here are our tips for keeping your weight down:

- **Buy light (but good quality) equipment** in the first place.
- **Don't take stuff that you won't use** – plan your trip carefully, draw up checklists, and stick to them.
- **Share gear** – if you're going in a pair or group, share your tent, portable stove, shampoo, toothpaste, first aid kit ... everything you can.
- **Take lightweight food** (see pages 81–83) and don't carry more water than you need.

- **Discard all unnecessary food packaging** (see page 88), but make sure you keep the cooking instructions.
- **Decant all liquids into plastic,** be they culinary or ablutionary – and only take the amount that you need.
- **Distribute the load amongst your party** – if you're a woman tramping with a man, make sure they carry *a lot* more than you.

There's an art to **packing your pack** – for both comfort and convenience. Divide your gear into 'departments', separated into plastic bags: clothing, food, cookery equipment, first aid kit, toiletries, etc. This will make things easier to pack and find (although there will always be some annoying rummaging around). It's always wise to double-bag your food, lest it spill and escape. Be sure to take plenty of plastic bags – they weigh hardly anything and you'll always need more than you predict.

Long items such as tents and roll mats should be packed first, although they can also be strapped to the outside. Pack heavy items towards the bottom, close to the spine, especially for steep terrain (this gives you a lower centre of gravity), and try to keep heavy items horizontally balanced. Make sure nothing nobbly is protruding into your back. Keep items you may need during the day at the top of your pack or in external pockets: an extra woolly or (heaven forbid) your raincoat, sunscreen, lunch, snacks and water. Be careful what you strap to the outside of the pack and make sure it is secure: it is liable to get wet, damaged or lost.

Pulling on a heavy pack is a strain. **Avoid injury** by donning it with care and attention. Loosen off the shoulder straps and hip belt a little. With the harness facing you, lift the pack on to one knee, or a nearby rock or log. Slide an arm through one side, and swing the pack gently on to your back. Slide the other arm through. Adjust the hip belt first, then the shoulders, and sternum. You can put the pack on while sitting down, but we recommend this method only if you have a friend to help you up (some gentlemen have been known to help their ladies put their pack on every time, bless 'em!).

Sleeping bags and mats

In the words of a famous New Zealand manufacturer of outdoor equipment: 'Adventurous spirits need a good night's sleep (so you can do it all again tomorrow).' Couldn't have said it better ourselves.

Sleeping bags

There are sleeping bags for all seasons, covering the extremes of equatorial high summer and the Arctic tundra. Seasonal averages vary distinctly from country to country, and in New Zealand we endure erratic and fast fluctuations, be it a sudden midsummer southerly snap, or an unusually mild winter month – four seasons in one day, as they say. So your first task is to **determine the temperature extremes you are likely to sleep in.**

All reputable brands of bag are tested and defined in terms of 'seasons', qualified by temperature, in accordance with European standards. These grades are:

SEASON	MINIMUM COMFORT TEMPERATURE (°C)	TYPICAL USES
1	+15	hot summer evenings
2	+5	spring and summer
3	-5	early spring to late autumn
3+	-10	all year round, low altitude
4/4+	-15/-20	cold winter climates and high elevations
5	-25 and below	high altitude mountaineering

In New Zealand conditions a 3–4 season bag should be sufficient – this will cover you down to about -15°c. In the summer months such a bag will be too hot, so make sure you buy one with a full-length zip so you can zip it open to cool off, or sleep in a bag liner instead (see page 33).

Once you've decided what seasonal range you require, the next decision is **fill**: down or synthetic. **Down** – soft, fine bird fluff, a fantastic natural insulator – offers a high warmth-to-weight ratio, resulting in a bag much lighter than synthetic fills of the same season rating. They are also much more compact. **Goose down** offers better insulation than **duck**, but duck down is still a good fill. It is the quantity of down that determines its warmth, so compare the grammage from bag to bag (usually 500–900 grams per square metre). Also, be aware that down bags are filled with different qualities and combinations of feather ('small feathers' are often added to the mix), and this will affect the **loft**: the ability of the down to expand and fill the space in the bag's **baffles** (the little compartments that stop the down from shifting and clumping). The disadvantage of down is that is prone to go soggy, flat and clumpy when wet, although some models have a water-resistant outer fabric – a worthwhile expense if you are likely to use the bag in damp conditions.

For those folk wanting a cheap, low-maintenance bag for warmer conditions, **synthetic fill** is a good option. These bags perform much better in the wet, retaining a good degree of insulation and drying much more quickly too. Synthetic bags are generally bulkier and heavier, so for longer trips and colder conditions, down is preferable.

Sleeping bags usually come in two **shapes**: mummy (or 'sarcophagus') and semi-rectangular, both with a draw-string hood. **Mummy bags** are great in colder temperatures, as they give a closer fit. With only one zip, and slightly less fabric and fill, they're lighter too. The **semi-rectangle** offers more room to move, and a separate foot zip for ventilation. The side zip can be completely undone and hey presto! – the bag is a duvet. Some models come with left and right zipper options, so you can zip two bags together and share with a friend. You can't beat a bit of extra body heat on a cold night!

Most manufacturers offer several **size** options too: longer, wider, and special shapes for women. Ask your retailer to check the catalogue and help you get the best fit.

The bag should come with a good **compression sack**, allowing you to squash it down to the size of a rugby ball.

Along your journey, **air the bag** as often as you can, but don't do what we did: popped it on the line outside the hut in brilliant morning sunshine, only to return at 4 p.m. after the rains came. (Thanks to Andrea and Christian who rescued it in the nick of time.) And watch out for kea: they are rather partial to a bit of bag-ripping along with their other acts of destruction.

If you **look after your sleeping bag** you should get years of use out of it. Down bags should be washed with care: follow any instructions provided or get some expert advice. Some manufacturers offer a professional bag cleaning service. Be wary of dry-cleaning, as detergents may be damaging. If you do wash your bag, handle it with great care – too much vigour will damage the baffles and it could develop cold spots. The best way to wash it is to gently agitate it in a bath with a non-detergent soap. Carefully squeeze out excess water and lay it flat to dry out a bit before hanging it on the line (heavy wet feathers may rip the baffles if hung up sodden). Down bags may also be dried in a large tumble drier on a low heat; pop in a tennis ball as well to stop the down clumping. Synthetic bags can be washed in the washing machine. Store bags uncompacted, hung over a coathanger or lightly stuffed into a pillowcase.

THE CASE OF THE DISAPPEARING SLEEPING BAG

We stretched out our fly on Kaweka Flats, the first chill of evening prickling the air with dampness. Paul laid out his huge arctic-strength sleeping bag on the ground-sheet. We all looked on enviously as he showed us the hood where you could stuff clothes to make a comfortable pillow. Daryl was particularly jealous, as he had only a thin, caravan-style sleeping bag. It was going to be a cold evening for Daryl, but none of us guessed how cold.

When darkness fell and dinner filled warm bellies, we prepared to doss down for the night. Everyone crawled into their sleeping bags, but Daryl couldn't find his anywhere. It had simply disappeared. We searched high and low, but it was gone – all we could find was a black jacket. Daryl spent a miserable night shivering between us, trying to sponge any heat he could.

In the morning Paul packed up his sleeping bag only to discover he'd stuffed Daryl's sleeping bag into the hood – mistaking it for his jacket. He'd been very cosy during the night with his arctic sleeping bag and Daryl's one as a pillow. The revelation had us all in fits of laughter, except for Daryl who was understandably still thawing out.

Shaun Barnett, in 'Tramping Moments of Near Disaster', *Wilderness*, November 1997

Sleeping bag liners

Cotton or silk sleeping bag liners are useful in several ways. First and foremost, they keep your sleeping bag clean: it's much easier to throw the liner in the washing machine than the bag, which can sustain damage with repeated washing. Secondly, they are great on hot nights: toss the bag aside and stay cool (while still keeping pesky mosquitoes at bay). Liners also provide a little extra warmth.

Pillows

For many, the extra weight of a small, compactable or inflatable pillow is a small price to pay for a good night's sleep (the lumpy rolled-up fleece will do, but is not ideal).

Sleeping mats

Sleeping on the ground is a challenge that many of us have never had to face, and those who haven't ever done it, or did it back in fourth form camp, may not realise that modern-day sleeping mats have revolutionised this previously cold and uncomfortable practice. This is good news for trampers. While you can usually be assured of a mattress in a hut, it isn't always guaranteed. And campers can forget the thin foam mattress or the cradle of ferns: tired old bones and sore muscles deserve better.

The market leader in sleeping mats is **Therm-a-Rest**, a self-inflating foam mattress. Lightweight and remarkably durable, they are surprisingly comfortable too. They come in several models and sizes, affording the usual trade-offs of weight, size, degree of comfort and price. They cost a pretty penny, and hardly ever go on sale, but they do come with a lifetime warranty. There are alternative self-inflatables: check the workmanship and guarantees, and buy from a reputable retailer.

Inflatable mats respond well to good care. First and foremost, don't strap it on to the outside of your pack or lay it on spiky terrain: it may get punctured. When you get home, wash it with warm soapy water, dry well, and store flat with the valve undone. You'll be sleeping soundly on it for many years to come – *maybe* even when you're over the hill!

A cheaper alternative is the **roll mat**, a closed-cell foam squab. These are adequate, but don't offer particularly good insulation or comfort. Tough nuts will manage with these quite well; softies will be tossing and turning all night.

Tents

New Zealand has such an excellent network of back-country huts you may never need to sleep in a tent. But for some of us, it's a choice rather than a requisite. You just can't beat the joys of tenting.

Tents are smart and fun. High-tech materials and improved designs mean they can be both remarkably weatherproof and superlightweight. A 1–2 person tent can be as light as 2 kilos. Tramping tents (as opposed to the palatial, multi-roomed family variety) come in more or less two shapes:

- **Tunnel**: these aerodynamically-shaped tents provide good wind resistance, and are therefore popular for exposed and alpine environments. Tunnel tents sit lower to the ground and have minimal headroom. However, when compared to other designs they afford greater floor area for weight.
- **Dome** or **geodesic**: this is a more spacious option, with better headroom than a tunnel – although of course you pay for that in weight. They tend to be more vulnerable in windy conditions, but they're better in the snow – their multi-pole construction providing a sturdier roof.

There are plenty of cheap tents on the market but as always, you get what you pay for. Look for a tent that's geared towards New Zealand conditions: think *rugged* and *rainfall.*

Look for these features, which good quality tents should have:

- **Double skin**: a vented inner sleeping area (i.e. breathable, with insect mesh panels or doors), and waterproof flysheet made from strong, tear-resistant lightweight synthetic materials. Let us emphasise **insect mesh**: this allows you to seal yourself up, away from sandflies and mozzies, while still allowing fresh air to flow through – a lifesaver on hot summer nights.
- A tough, **built-in groundsheet** in a 'tub' shape: the sheet comes up a good 15 centimetres off the ground to protect you from puddles and ricochet raindrops.
- **Double-stitched and sealed seams**, for improved waterproofing and tear resistance.
- **Lightweight poles**, usually aluminium alloy in multiple sections joined by elastic shock cord.

Beyond this, it's all about space. How much room do you need and are you prepared to carry the extra weight for it? Remember, it's not all about you: your gear needs shelter too. Look for a tent with sufficient vestibule space at one or both ends for storing your pack, boots and other equipment. Vestibule space is also invaluable in a relentless downpour, allowing you to cook out of the rain. *Never* cook inside the tent!

For some trampers, a **flysheet** will suffice as a lightweight shelter. This is a single layer only, and is adequate for most conditions below the bushline. Some models of double-skin tent allow you to pitch the fly on its own.

Before you buy your tent, ask your retailer to show you how to pitch it. Then have a go yourself, at home in the backyard or at the park – don't wait till you get to camp to discover you're not quite sure how it goes up. Fumbling with an unfamiliar tent is horrible in the wind and rain (and should anyone be around, you'll look like a complete fool!).

TENT TIPS

- Where possible, **stay at established campsites.** This reduces your impact on the environment.
- **Check out the lie of the land.** Flat ground is obviously good, and grassy ground will provide some additional comfort. A slightly elevated site is always best; that'll save you waking up in a puddle if it rains all night.
- Pitching under a tree may seem like a good idea, providing shelter and a windbreak, but be careful. Branches may snap off on stormy nights, or you may even get struck by lightning. **Camp only under friendly looking trees, or well out from under them.**
- **Never camp too close to the edge of a river or stream.** If water levels rise in the night you may get swept away.
- If you're going to make a **campfire**, be sure to position your tent upwind of it (or your fire downwind of the tent). For more on fire safety, see page 99.
- **Peg your tent out with gusto.** A big wind *will* whip up in the night. If the ground's too hard for pegs, secure the guy lines with rocks or around a tree.
- A well-erected tent should look proud and taut. A saggy tent is a smaller tent, and much more vulnerable to the wind. **Adjust the tension via the guy ropes and pegs.**
- If possible, **pack your tent up dry.** It will weigh less, and be much more inviting when unpacked the next evening (especially if you arrive after sundown). On dewy mornings, leave it in the sun for another half an hour if time allows, or use a bandana to mop up some drops. And whenever the sun shines, take the opportunity to air out the tent and its contents.

- A well-used tent will get the worse for wear, so **hang on to the repair kit** that came with it: this usually consists of fabric patches, pole repair sleeve and occasionally seam sealer. Or carry a roll of duct tape – it'll temporarily fix just about anything (even snorers).

A TENT ON THE FLY

Big Daddy, Frazer and I ascended the Thunder Glacier in a white out. Finding a flattish snowslope near the head of the Olivine Ice Plateau, we set up my beloved tent. The morning after dawned fine and clear, with stunning views to enjoy. As I stood on Key Rock taking photos, I heard a sudden yell. Turning around I saw the tent, still fully erect, dance airborne over the nearby bluff and vanish out of sight. Frazer, having pulled out the tent pegs, was putting them in the peg bag when a rogue puff of wind – on an otherwise perfectly calm morning – had wafted the tent over the edge. We looked over to see the tent gracefully glissading on its roof down a steep snow slope above bluffs. The tent caught for a moment, then disappeared into a gut.

My partners were assigned to retrieval, and descended – much like the tent – out of sight. A couple of hours later they returned to report that although initially nowhere to be seen, it suddenly blew out of a gully and continued its merry dance across the slope toward another bluff. Sprinting across lumpy avalanche debris, Frazer just managed to catch the tent before it dropped over the edge.

The tent had fallen some 600 vertical metres but was remarkably intact, sporting merely cuts and grazes on its roof. We patched these with duct tape and continued on.

Kelvin Lloyd

The lightweight alternative to the tent, popular with climbers, solo trampers and minimalists, is the **cocoon** or **bivvy bag**. These offer true 'freedom camping' as you can sleep just about anywhere. They range from waterproof shells that slip over a sleeping bag to slightly more roomy shelters that look like a cross between a sleeping bag and a one-person tent – there is little or no room for your gear. Besides being claustrophobic and unsociable, these rig-ups tend to suffer from condensation, so buy one in Gore-Tex or another breathable fabric.

Cooking gear

Cooking equipment can be heavy and bulky, but need not be. If you buy the right kit, pack only the necessaries, and pool resources where possible, you can keep weight to a minimum and still have everything you need to make a decent meal.

Portable stoves

Overnight trampers will almost always need to take their own portable stove. While most huts have a place for you to cook, very few provide facilities beyond a bench and a sink. Weary walkers need hot food. There's nothing more restorative than several cups of hot tea followed by a big, fat, piping-hot pot of grub.

There are several types of portable stove, each offering different benefits and ranging widely in price. We all have our favourite, so ask around your friends or tramping acquaintances – what do they use and why? Whichever you choose, ask the salesperson to demonstrate it for you. Better still, have a go yourself. Make sure you've mastered the art of using it before you go bush.

Always check that your stove is in **working order** before you pack it. Also make sure you have something to light it with – a lighter, and plenty of matches for backup.

GAS STOVES

Typical brands are MSR, Primus, Kovea and Coleman. Fuel is a butane/propane mix, which comes in a self-resealable canister. Be sure to buy one with a standard thread: not all models take all brands of canister.

PROS

- inexpensive (most under $100)
- easy to use
- quick on the boil
- lightweight, sometimes super-lightweight
- fuel canister can also be used for a lantern
- gas is safely contained

CONS

- fuel is relatively expensive
- less effective in cold and high altitude conditions
- environmental impact: canisters cannot be refilled
- high centre of gravity, some degree of topple risk

LIQUID FUEL STOVES

Typical brands are MSR, Primus, Optimus and Coleman. The fuel, known as white spirit, is available from outdoor stores (Coleman fuel), and from major service stations: Britolite (BP), Calite (Caltex), Pegasol AA (Mobil) and Shellite (Shell). Multi-fuel models are available (e.g. they can run on kerosene, petrol, diesel and methylated spirits) but you have to switch the jets (they come with two). These stoves, however, run more efficiently on white spirit so that's your best bet.

PROS

- efficient in cold conditions
- quick on the boil
- economical fuel user
- canisters can be refilled

CONS

- more expensive than gas models ($150–300)
- fuel is highly volatile
- the unit needs priming and ongoing general maintenance (e.g. cleaning jets, replacing valve and washer)

METHYLATED SPIRIT STOVES

Most common brand is Trangia. Fuel is methylated spirits, widely available from outdoor and hardware stores, service stations and supermarkets.

PROS

- easy to use
- safest option – low volatility fuel and a stable cooking set up
- fuel readily available
- wind-proof and fail-proof – it always works

CONS

- weight – the heaviest of all the options
- bulky
- least efficient – uses the most fuel
- low heat output – slow to boil

The amount of **fuel required** depends on many factors, including how many people you're cooking for, what you're cooking, altitude and weather conditions. When starting out it's best to take more than you need: as time goes on you'll learn to estimate quantities better. However, if you're feeling particularly eager you can test your stove in advance by seeing how many times you can boil up the billy on one tank or half a tank of fuel. Fuel savings can be made by partially cooking food and allowing it to finish off under its own steam (we often leave our half-cooked rice or pasta to stand while we're making the sauce).

Take extra care with portable stoves, especially in enclosed spaces. *Never* use a stove in a tent, and always make sure you have adequate ventilation in huts. See pages 80–91 for more on camp cookery.

Please note that stoves and canisters containing fuel – and sometimes even those that have contained fuel – cannot be taken on commercial aircraft.

Cooking pots

If you're tramping alone, one pot (known to trampers as a *billy*) should be sufficient for your needs. You can eat directly from the billy or its lid, so that'll save you the weight of a plate. For two people we recommend two pots. Not only does this increase your scope for camp menus, but also it enables you to brew a cup of tea while the noodles are on. For larger groups, do the maths. More pots or larger pots: it's all about capacity.

The best billies on the market are titanium, a lightweight alloy that is durable but rather expensive. Aluminium is also light, and cheap, but a bugger to clean. Hard-anodised aluminium is an increasingly popular alternative. Though a little heavier, stainless steel is more durable and easier to clean, but doesn't conduct heat consistently and can burn food. We do not recommend non-stick camping cookwear.

Whichever you choose, it should have a close-fitting lid and a sound handle or pot-grab. A dedicated stuff sac is useful too, for it will soon be caked in soot!

> You'll find a comprehensive **equipment checklist** at the back of this book.

Plates, cups and cutlery

A variety of bowls, cups and cutlery is available – stainless steel, aluminium, enamel and plastics such as polypropylene. It comes down to personal preference; while some may weigh a little more, some of us just can't drink a cuppa out of plastic.

You may want to eat straight out of your pot, ideal in cold conditions as it keeps your food hot. Otherwise take a plate, or better still a **bowl** – there tends to be some sloshing about.

Cutlery can be kept to a minimum. A spoon and a penknife may be sufficient, although a fork may be necessary for noodles. Lexan polycarbonate is great, claimed by its manufacturers to be 'break-resistant' – it's certainly hardwearing and lightweight. Titanium cutlery is also available, although the amount of weight saved is minimal and the cost quite high. An entirely acceptable option is lightweight cutlery out of your kitchen drawer.

The tramper's **knife** has many uses, besides just slicing salami. But unless you're hunting pigs, a penknife (e.g. Swiss Army) or multi-tool (e.g. Leatherman) will suffice. Not only will it allow you to cut your lunch and open tins, you can also trim your nails, tweeze your prickle, and conduct other repairs to person and equipment. Don't leave home without it.

Whilst the multi-feature Swiss Army knives and Leathermans are impressive, do you really need a magnifying glass or ruler on the track? As long as your knife has a quality blade, a tin opener, scissors and maybe a saw-blade, it should be adequate.

Washing up

At the end of your meals, wash your dishes in the hut sink or, if there are no facilities, draw water from the source and wash them well away from it. A **pot scourer** and small amount of **dishwashing liquid** will be indispensable – especially if you're washing up in cold water. A handful of sand makes an adequate scourer if you get stuck.

Water bottles

A good quality water bottle is an essential part of your kit. Although there may be potable water supplies along the track, they may be few and far between. Always carry sufficient drinking water supplies with you, (see pages 89–91 for more on water).

There are three main types of water container:

- hard plastic (e.g. polycarbonate)
- stainless steel
- bladder with bite valve (e.g. CamelBak)

Do not rely on soft drink bottles. They are liable to split, leak or leach decaying plastic residues.

Torches and lanterns

Except on failsafe day trips, every member of your group should carry their own torch. Even if you plan to do everything during daylight hours, remember that once the sun goes down, you're in the dark. Pitch dark. In unfamiliar territory, amongst unknown hazards – obstacles, potholes and bluffs, spider-filled long-drops. If you do not have a working torch, you are putting yourself in danger (a spider could bite your bottom!).

Besides the obvious benefit of enabling you to see in the dark, a torch can also serve as a beacon for would-be rescuers.

The best and most popular torch for trampers is the **headlamp**. These lightweight torches are primarily LED, and strap comfortably on top of your head, offering the decided advantage of being hands-free and always illuminating the spot where you're looking (beware of dazzling your companions though). Headlamps can be quite costly; there are plenty of inexpensive **handheld** torches around – look for something compact, lightweight but sufficiently powerful.

LED bulbs generally do not need replacing during the life of the headlamp, and this is one of the reasons they have taken over from halogens. The other is that their batteries last longer. With all torches, **check that it is working** before you set off, and irrespective of how new it is, **always carry spare batteries and bulbs.**

For an ambient light, consider a **lantern.** Their radiant glow and modest heat output provides a welcome, round-the-campfire atmosphere, offering warming reassurance to those with a little bush-fright. They are a bit heavy, especially by the time you add extra fuel and batteries, so should probably only be considered for short, group trips. Don't ever use a gas lantern in your tent – naked flames don't belong in a tent.

So, that means no **candles** in the tent either, please – and you'll be lucky to keep one lit outside. Huts are a different matter: candles are encouraged. They throw a soothing, rosy glow over the room – you'll forget all about the grime and mice.

At the end of the night, don't forget to **blow out your candles** and **extinguish your fire**: the unattended flame can be dangerous. For more on fire safety, see page 99.

LIGHTWEIGHT LUXURIES

Enhance your enjoyment by taking a few of your favourite things (as long as they weigh next to nothing):

- deck of cards or travel games (Scrabble, chess, etc.)
- a paperback book
- MP3 player, battery-powered, not rechargeable
- whisky, decanted into a plastic bottle
- freshly ground coffee
- extra special sweet treats
- candles
- hacky sack or frisbee

Toilet gear

This isn't the catwalk. You don't need your hairdryer, and you certainly don't need your lipstick. Consider yourself liberated.

This is what we suggest you take:

- bio-degradable soap
- toothbrush and toothpaste
- pack towel (a small microfibre towel available from tramping shops, highly absorbent, super-quick-drying and lightweight)
- small quantity of moisturiser or barrier cream
- sun block and lip salve
- insect repellent (see pages 67–68)
- muscle rub/liniment (e.g. Tiger Balm)
- deodorant, if you must
- toilet paper or tissues

While you're at it, don't forget your first aid and emergency kit.

First aid and emergency kit

Basic first aid skills are useful for everyone, not just for those going bush. However, if you intend going tramping in remote areas or in challenging terrain, first aid skills become even more important – there may be no one else to help. Consider taking one of the first aid courses offered by the Mountain Safety Council – they are tailored specifically for the outdoor environment. St John's and the Red Cross also offer courses, or read a book: there are first aid manuals at your local library.

Always take at least a basic first aid kit with you on your trip (groups may take one between them). It could contain:

- plasters and blister plasters or rings
- bandages (triangular and crepe) and safety pins
- sterile gauze pads and wound dressings

- adhesive tape
- antiseptic cream
- antihistamine tablets or cream
- painkillers, e.g. aspirin, paracetamol, Voltaren
- disposable gloves
- rehydration powders, e.g. Gastrolyte or Enerlyte (see pages 69–70)
- survival bag (also known as an **emergency blanket;** the Mountain Safety Council one is ideal – it has survival tips printed on it)
- whistle (for attracting attention)

WHAT YOU SHOULD HAVE LEFT AT HOME

Even the most experienced trampers will still pack a thing or two they don't use, but some people make overpacking an art. And how they struggle under the weight of their packs, and how we glance askance at them in the hut, giggling at their foolishness. Here are some things we thought our fellow trampers could have left at home:

- 4 kilo barbecue gas cylinder (party member was asked to bring 'gas' for the camp stove)
- six-pack of cola
- huge bottle of Evian – in Fiordland
- 3 litres of fresh milk
- hardback edition of *The Da Vinci Code*
- hairdryer
- wheely suitcase

Optional extras

You can, of course, take any extras you like, but resist the temptation to take too much – it all adds to your pack weight. Some useful items you might consider are:

- binoculars
- camera
- field guides (small paperbacks ideally, or photocopy out the relevant pages) – for identifying flora and fauna (see *Further Reading* at the back of the book)
- walking (e.g. Leki) stick
- fire-starters (for damp conditions)
- laundry soap and elastic washing line
- mobile telephone (see page 103)
- GPS (see page 66)
- small sewing kit (needle and thread) for minor repairs

The art of walking

The secret to pleasurable tramping – especially when you're starting out – is to **be prepared** and **know your limits**. If you're new to tramping, you may not know what your limits are.

New Zealand offers magnificent tramping for walkers of all abilities, and it's important that you choose a tramp that you can safely complete – *and enjoy*. Key things to consider are **distance, elevation change,** and the type of **terrain**. Are you fit enough for it? And have you got the right gear for the conditions?

A good place to start is at your nearest Department of Conservation (DOC) *Te Papa Atawhai* visitor centre. DOC is responsible for conserving the natural and historic heritage of New Zealand, and manages the 14 national parks and 24 conservation/forest parks that make up the 'conservation estate', covering nearly one-third of the country. DOC field staff also maintain thousands of kilometres of tracks and huts for us to enjoy, and provide information on facilities and conditions. It's worth checking with them for updates on track and weather conditions before setting off on your tramp (see page 50). Many city and regional councils and private operators also maintain a network of graded and signposted tracks.

Find out about the walks in your area. Pamphlets and maps abound, as do books on the subject: turn to *Further Reading* at the end of this book for just a handful.

To enjoy tramping from day one, start with gentle day walks and build up to overnighters and beyond. Stay inside your limit, and push it out gently. Don't blow your chances of becoming a happy tramper by biting off more than you can chew. One bad experience could put you off for life.

Physical challenge is as much a part of tramping as a bag of scroggin. Feeling a bit tired and sore at the end of a day's walk is a badge of honour, a reminder of your achievement. Did I really walk all that way?

But if you push the limits, expect to pay the price. Too far, too fast, ill-prepared or beyond your skill level – tramping can become very hard indeed: exhausting, frightening and unsafe.

For all but the most short and urban walkways, it's best to tramp with a friend or in a group. This is especially important for new trampers. It's safer, more fun, and the more experienced of the party can share their knowledge and skills. Consider joining one of New Zealand's many tramping or alpine clubs. This an excellent way to learn the art of tramping quickly and safely. As well as leading trips into the bush, clubs hold regular meetings and skills courses, and offer camaraderie in the company of like-minded people. The Federated Mountain Clubs' website has a comprehensive list of clubs nationwide (www.fmc.org.nz).

> **I WAS SOMEWHAT DUBIOUS** about the merits of tramping clubs, fearing an enclave of bushily bearded men in too short shorts racing one another over distant ranges, but in reality, joining one took me further and gave me experiences I'd never have had going bush on my own. I found myself in the company of experienced trampers who had a wealth of bushcraft wisdom to share, and they led me off the beaten track into wilderness areas I initially wouldn't have had the confidence to explore otherwise. Because the tramping club had a gear library, belonging to one also meant I could borrow things like crampons and billies until I was ready to invest in my own kit.
>
> Polly Greeks

DEPARTMENT OF CONSERVATION TRACK GRADINGS

DOC's walks range from the short and very easy to the remote and difficult. They are keen to see you stay within your limits, and grade all tracks so you know what to expect. Starting from easy to hard, they are:

- **Short walk** – well formed, easy walking.
- **Walking track** – well formed, easy longer walks.
- **Great Walk and Easy tramping track** – formed track for comfortable overnight tramping trips. All rivers will be bridged.
- **Tramping track** – mostly unformed but with track directional markers, poles or cairns. May require unbridged river crossings.
- **Route** – unformed, suitable only for experienced people with good back-country skills.

Check out track gradings in advance on DOC's website (www.doc.govt.nz); you can check out hut locations, facilities and fees while you're at it, too.

Weather and track conditions

Keep your fingers crossed for clear, blue skies because bad weather is the big spoiler. It is vital that you are always prepared for all possible weather conditions. New Zealand's weather can change very quickly, especially near the mountains where cloud is wont to hang about.

Obtaining an up to date weather forecast is an essential part of your pre-trip planning. While it might not always tell you what you want to know (endless sunshine, a light cooling breeze and a temperature of 20°c), it will tell you what you need to know. If the weather's going to be wet, you may want to take extra plastic bags and some more socks. If there's going to be a heatwave, you might decide to set off extra early to avoid the midday sun. But more importantly, a weather forecast will tell you if extreme conditions are on the way, and in this scenario, you may wish to delay or even cancel your trip. Flash flooding and rising river levels are dangerous, as are high winds or heavy snows.

For trips on tracks that are prone to experience changeable conditions, we recommend you **have a Plan B up your sleeve**. If Plan A isn't viable, perhaps there's another track nearby you can do instead? Or maybe there's an alternative river crossing to the one you planned to take? It would be a shame to cancel your trip after all the planning that went into it.

Weather forecasts are readily available and on the whole they are pretty accurate. However, they vary in detail such as geographical coverage and time frame.

- For the most current and detailed local forecasts, contact **MetService** – www.metservice.co.nz or tel 0900-999 + your area code. They also offer a fax or email service.
- **Television forecasts** (especially on the six o'clock news) provide short- and long-range information, nationally and by region. They are particularly good at showing you what's brewing for the next few days.
- **Radio New Zealand** (101 FM) broadcasts detailed regional forecasts after the news on the hour. In addition they provide a long-range forecast just after 1 p.m., a mountain forecast after 4 p.m., and two coastal forecasts after 5 p.m. and 3 a.m.
- Victoria University's **Weather and Climate Service** website – www.metvuw.com – presents frequently updated weather data including satellite and radar imagery. It is particularly useful for predicting rain.

UNDERSTANDING WEATHER FORECASTS

If you've not paid much attention to the weather before, you may not be familiar with weather maps and meteorological terms. Here are some basics:

FRONTS Fronts mark boundaries between air of different temperatures and origin, and are places where upward air motion occurs. These are cold fronts, where cold air is advancing and replacing warm air.

ISOBARS Isobars join places where air pressure is the same. The numbers on the isobars are the air pressure measured in hectoPascals (hPa).

HIGHS Highs are areas of high air pressure, associated with sinking air, and marked with an 'H'.

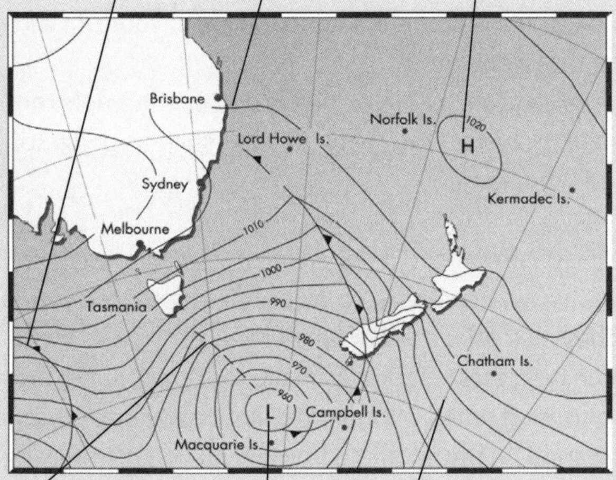

TROUGH An area of low pressure extending away from a low, frequently containing thunderstorms and showers. Marked by a dashed line.

LOW Lows are areas of low air pressure, associated with rising air, and marked with an 'L'.

WIND The pattern of the isobars tells you what the wind is doing at different places – the wind mostly blows parallel to the isobars. Generally, the closer the isobars, the stronger the wind and in the Southern Hemisphere the wind blows clockwise around a low, and anticlockwise around a high.

Taken from Erick Brenstrum's *New Zealand Weather Book*, great if you want to know how New Zealand's weather works.

- Most **newspapers** have a good weather page, accurate at the time of going to print.
- For longer trips, you could consider taking a **Mountain Radio Service** (MRS) receiver. The Service broadcasts weather forecasts daily (see page 103).

Once you're on the track, **keep an eye on the weather.** With practice, you can become adept at predicting weather in the short term, although if you're walking in a valley, hills and mountains will limit this. A clear sky with high cloud will generally indicate favourable conditions. Dark sky and low cloud normally means rain. Gauging the degree between the two, looking towards your direction of travel and that of the weather, can enable you to predict what's going to happen in the next few hours.

Weather conditions can change very quickly and this can put you in danger. Watch for mist or low cloud that starts creeping into your path – it can disorientate you in mere moments, a common cause of getting lost. And be particularly wary of rain clouds on the horizon if you've got river crossings coming up.

Chances are you can't outrun the weather, but always **be prepared for the unexpected** and ensure that everyone in your group is adequately equipped. If you do get caught in bad weather, don't be afraid to turn back or take shelter. You'll find tips for surviving extreme conditions on pages 102–12.

The weather will affect the **track conditions** (and therefore the time needed to complete it). Tracks that are a breeze in the dry can be transformed into a treacherous ordeal in the wet. Yesterday's weather can affect you too: heavy rain or snowmelt may have swollen rivers and streams or created a quagmire, while a big storm may have littered the track with debris and treefall.

Are you prepared for all eventualities? Do what you can to anticipate the conditions, and don't set out unless you know you can handle it.

There are several ports of call for getting updates on track conditions:

- For **DOC** tracks, check in with the nearest **visitor centre**. They not only have information on current conditions, but you can get detailed weather forecasts there while you're at it.
- The **Visitor Information Network** is also a helpful resource. They will either hold up to date information, or direct you to it.
- Some of the best expert advice on local track conditions can be found at **local tramping clubs**. For a list of these, visit www.fmc.org.nz.

It rained and rained and rained and rained
the average was well maintained
and when the tracks had turned to bogs
it started raining cats and dogs

After a drought of half an hour
we had a most refreshing shower
and then the most curious thing of all
a gentle rain began to fall

Next day but one was mostly dry
apart from a deluge from the sky
which wet our party to the skin
and after that, the rain set in

Anonymous

Walking skills

If you're expecting a walk in the park, go to the park. New Zealand tramping can be tough, but there are ways to make it easier. At the risk of teaching you to suck eggs, here are some tips.

The best to way to pick up tramping skills is to go with an experienced person or better still, a group. Whoever you go with, be prepared to take responsibility for yourself: only ever set off if you are confident *you* can go the distance. Solo trampers need to be especially self-reliant.

Remember that you'll be walking a lot further in a day than you usually would, possibly *all* day – with a great big pack on your back. **Stamina**, not speed, is the key. So firstly, expect to walk quite a bit slower than normal. The secret to enjoyable tramping is to settle into your own **pace**; you'll be amazed how far your natural rhythm will take you. Remember the tortoise and the hare?

Despite the fact that walking slowly is unequivocally safer, and you also see more, racing on ahead is very common. This sometimes ends in tears. You will tire more quickly and increase the risk of injury and accidents. You will also miss opportunities to stop and smell the Ti tree. If you have the time, take it. **'Being' in the outdoors is the essence of the tramper's journey.**

Walking at your own pace becomes a bit more tricky in a group. It is, however, very important that the group sticks together – not necessarily easy to do when the super-fit show-offs invariably surge on ahead while the stragglers struggle to catch up, pooped and disheartened. A good group dynamic is therefore highly desirable. For starters, the subject of speed should be totally avoided. Talk instead in terms of *expectations* – where you're going to get to and by when – and make sure these goals are realistic and well-managed.

The ideal tramping party will be led by an experienced, mature and considerate person who will start the group off slowly, watching and talking to individuals and accordingly settling the group into a pace ideal for everyone. If no such leader is evident, you may have to seize the mantle yourself. Move to the front, reign in the jocks, and moderate the pace. This will have a positively transformative effect on the group.

Frequent **rest stops** are vital – five minutes each hour is a good rule of thumb. The harder your tramp, the more important the rest. Not only does your body need this time to relax and refuel, but rest stops serve as an encouraging mental milestone during a tough struggle. ('I'll walk another half an hour then have a break.') Pick a nice spot, stop and take the weight off your feet (for short stops you needn't even take your pack off – just prop yourself up against a tree). Have a drink and something to eat.

A reasonable level of physical fitness is a sound platform for the new tramper, however there are many tips and tricks that will make it even safer, easier and more enjoyable:

- **Rise and shine at daybreak.** That way you'll have a whole day's worth of light in which to reach your destination – a particularly useful way to avoid stress if it takes you a bit longer than you expect. You'll also have more time to rest and potter about.
- Ensure you are **comfortable**. Check your boots and pack *before* you start – are they adjusted for the best fit? Are you warm or cool enough?
- When you start out, take it easy and allow your body to gently **warm up**. Don't worry if your pace is a bit slow to begin with; you'll soon oil up and find your rhythm.
- Aim to maintain a **steady pace**. If you're getting really puffed, you're probably pushing it too hard. If the terrain is physically challenging, slow down – shift into a lower gear.
- Keep an eye on the track, and **pick the easiest path** for you. It's not necessary to follow the exact footfalls of the person ahead.

- **Be prepared to get your feet wet.** While your instincts may tell you to doff the boots and attempt a barefoot clamber, this seldom pays dividends. For a start it will be harder, with slip-overs and foot bash-ups not infrequent. But you can bet your bottom dollar there will be another river to cross, probably just round the corner. Better to plough on through and be done with it. Wet feet? Worse things have happened at sea!
- When you encounter **uneven or slippery terrain**, take extra care. Focus on maintaining good balance and a sure grip underfoot. Grab handholds where you can.
- **Be careful not to topple.** Wearing a heavy pack alters your centre of gravity, something that becomes more apparent on steep terrain. After time, your body will naturally adjust (and you'll get stronger if you tramp often enough), but until then remember that a fully-laden pack can tip you over the edge.
- Allow adequate time for **rest stops** but beware of taking too long: your muscles may stiffen up and it will be a struggle to get going again. In cool conditions, consider popping on an extra layer while you're stationary to conserve vital body heat.

A WORD OF ADVICE ON GOING UPHILL: the worst, absolutely the worst thing you can do is be thinking about the hill itself. Talk to your companions (if you have the breath), stir up an argument, or hum a song. Take an inordinate interest in plant succession as you climb higher or listen out for birds. If you have the meditative ability to follow your companion's heels and empty your mind of all thoughts entirely, then do it – but don't think about the hill.

Mark Pickering, in *The Hills*, 1988

River crossings

If you are tramping on well-used paths or easy DOC tracks, you may never to have face a dangerous river crossing. However, crossing rivers and streams – on foot, that is, not over a bridge – is often part of the New Zealand outdoor experience and presents one of the most serious risks to trampers, usually resulting in several deaths each year. That's because a fast-flowing stream, not even knee-deep, can sweep you clean off your feet. In order to stay safe, you need to know how to cross – or whether you should even attempt it.

Imagine reaching a river or stream only to discover that it is faster and deeper than you expected due to recent rainfall.

- Your initial reaction may be that you *have* to get to the other side. Do you really? Perhaps you can **retrace your steps or sit it out** in the hut from whence you came. Some rivers may be impassable for only a few hours; others for several days.
- Perhaps it *is* crossable. How will you know? **Look out for these warning signs**: discoloured, surging water; the sound of rolling boulders; and debris being carried along the flow. If you see these signs the answer is no.
- Every river crossing needs to be evaluated. Whether you cross will depend not only on the river conditions, but also the **strength, skill and experience** of you and your group.
- **Survey possible crossing points.** Look for the slowest, shallowest and usually therefore the widest part of the river. Narrow, fast-flowing channels should be avoided. Make sure there are easy entry and exit points.
- **Crossings are always best made in a group** – should you slip or fall your companions will hold you up. (See opposite.)
- **Never attempt to cross a river alone** unless it is absolutely safe for you to do so. (See page 60.)
- **Don't take your boots off.**

Crossing the river in a group

Always cross the river in a group if you can: if you slip or lose your grip, your companions can support you. There is fervent debate amongst the tramping fraternity as to the best method for crossing in a group, and here we present our two preferred methods (as recommended by the Mountain Safety Council):

1. First, **line up the people in your group** according to their level of strength and experience:
   - a strong person at the upstream end of the line
   - the strongest, most experienced person alongside them for extra support
   - another strong person at the downstream end
   - the rest of the group in between.
2. **Undo pack chest straps** and **loosen shoulder straps,** but **keep waist belts done up.**
3. **EITHER** each member then inserts their arms between their neighbour's pack and their back, and grasps either their waist belt or their pack shoulder strap (down low) on the opposite side. This is the preferred variation, especially in deep water;

   OR each member inserts their arms between their neighbour's pack and their back, and grasps their pants or shorts on the opposite side at hip level. Ensure the grasp encompasses the belt or waistband that holds up the pants or shorts. This variation is suitable for straightforward crossings where the river is knee to mid-thigh deep and the current is weak.
4. **In either case,** the group should then move into the river as a single unit, in line with the flow of the current – the strongest person upstream and therefore bearing the brunt of the flow.

Crossing the river on your own

If you are alone and a solo crossing is unavoidable, this technique will give you considerable support and is particularly helpful if the bottom is slippery.

1. Find a pole (e.g. a branch) about two metres in length and comfortable to grasp. Ensure it is strong enough to support your weight. Use your Leki stick if you have one.
2. Hold the pole in both hands diagonally across the front of your body.
3. Push the lower end into the riverbed about a metre upstream from your feet.
4. Lean on the prop as a 'third leg' to balance as you move each foot forward. Move only one leg at a time, planting it firmly before moving on; maintain two points of contact at all times.
5. When both feet are securely placed, move the pole forward and push it into the riverbed again. Move the pole through, not over, the water.
6. If you need to retreat then reverse your grip on the pole and turn yourself around (facing upstream) until you are ready to move back the way you came.

If you get swept away

If you do get swept away, stay calm. Adopt the river-float position: on your back, feet facing downstream. Pull your shoulder straps tight to stop your pack riding above your head. Use your arms to guide yourself to the nearest bank or into calmer water.

A dramatic mishap in a river will drain your strength. It is usually best to stop and make a hot drink, change into dry clothes, and possibly camp early.

AS FAR AS TRAMPING TRIPS GO, this one was meant to be easy, just a leisurely overnight stroll into the Tararuas.

As forecasted, Dave and I encountered a couple of showers while we made our way through the bush, but the river was still flowing clearly by the time we reached its banks in the late afternoon. Several other parties had beaten us there and set up in the hut, so we decided to tramp on to a smaller hut over the river. Despite the overcast sky, neither of us gave a moment's thought to getting back the next day.

We found a spot to cross the river, unclipped our pack waistbelts and linked arms before shuffling into the water. It was surprisingly swift and far deeper than we realised. One moment we were wading through mid-thigh water, the next we were in over our heads and being swept downstream. It was quite hard not to panic but eventually we made it over to the other bank, about 100 metres down from where we had entered the river.

We found the other hut and dried off, just as the heavens opened. The rain thundered down on the tin roof all night and was still bucketing down the next morning when we discovered the river was well and truly in flood. Crossing it was unthinkable.

Luckily we met a pair of pig hunters and their dogs who knew the region very well and they led us back out, but it was an all-day mission of bush-bashing, followed by a long trudge along unsealed roads in the torrential rain to reach the car.

Polly Greeks

Navigation

Once you venture beyond gentle walkways and urban nature trails, it is easy to lose your way. This is the back country. Tracks can be hard to follow; blending in with surroundings or becoming overgrown. Dense forest or unexpected mist may leave you without a sense of direction. Crossroads abound – are you sure you're taking the right turn?

Navigation is an essential part of the tramper's journey: where are you going, how are you going to get there, and where are you now? A map and compass will go a long way in keeping you on the right track, but you need more than that. Your powers of observation and gut instincts may well be called upon too. Make all your navigational decisions good ones – you're a long, long way from home.

See pages 102–12 for tips on getting lost and being found again.

Map and compass

A map is an essential part of your kit for all but the shortest and well-signposted strolls:

- Use the map to **plan your walk:** anticipate not only distance but changes in elevation and terrain too.
- On the track, **pinpoint your location** by identifying landmarks, such as water sources, peaks, bluffs and bridges. This also indicates your route onward.
- **Gauge your progress** as you walk – how far have you gone and how far have you got to go?

There are two types of topographical map available, and which one you choose is dependent on the degree of difficulty of your tramp:

- The **Parkmap** series (generally on a scale of 1:100,000) covers large areas – often a whole national park. The maps are

useful for trip planning and an adequate guide for easy, well-signposted tracks.
- **Terralink** produces a series of detailed maps (1:50,000) for the whole country, and also a set conveniently tailored to popular 'recreation areas'. These give you all the geographical features you need to be aware of, as well as easy-to-read topographical lines so you can see the ups and downs. They are a must for any tramp other than the most well-trodden.

If you haven't used these sorts of maps before, take the time to familiarise yourself with them. Don't be overwhelmed by the super-fine detail and symbols – maps *are* fun ... at least until you have to fold them up again. On the track, make sure everyone in your party has ready access to the map and knows how to read it. Each time you stop, get the map out and work out where you are on it. A plastic map pouch, available from outdoor stores and some DOC visitor centres, will protect it from the rain.

If you stick to well-marked trails you may never need to use a **compass**. However, should you graduate to 'off-track' tramping (that is, you're following routes rather than tracks), a compass will become essential.

You don't need to spend a lot of money on a compass: even the cheap ones still point north. What is important is that you know how to use it, and that you are carrying it when you need it. The 'Silva'-type compass is the most popular. Most are made of clear durable plastic with the compass housing offset to the side. The base often has an in-built magnifying glass and various scales etched into it that will aid with map reading and distance measurement.

> **OFTEN THE BIGGEST NAVIGATIONAL BLUNDERS** come through over-confidence and failing to check the map, because you were sure you knew where you were.
>
> Mark Pickering, in *The Hills*, 1988

You can learn navigation and orienteering skills at various clubs including the Scouts (perhaps it's too late for you?), or tramping and mountaineering clubs, often as part of a 'bushcraft' course. Otherwise, your local library will probably hold a book or two on the subject. Trevor Burgess's book *Don't Die in the Bush* offers a good basic introduction; the book is fairly readily available and written specifically for New Zealand conditions.

Follow the markers

Many of New Zealand's popular walkways are so well trodden that you couldn't lose them if you wanted to. However, this isn't the case for most tracks, and that's why you must follow the markers. Now this may seem obvious, and easy, but you may actually find it is not. It's quite common to be distracted by good conversation or some sort of surprise – such as a landslide or treefall on the track, or a desire to take a dip in the lake. The person up front, in particular, must keenly observe the way ahead and move forward from marker to marker.

Markers are usually an orange plastic triangle, but can also take the form of metal rectangles (known as **permolats**), metal discs and the odd cairn (often on riverbeds or above the bushline). Sometimes you'll see bits of ribbon or pink triangles, but be wary of following these: more often that not they're there for someone else, such as DOC field staff.

If you lose the markers, stop immediately. With luck you'll be tramping with a buddy: one person should stay put while the other retraces your steps in an attempt to pick up the markers again (the theory being that the stay-put person is so far only slightly lost and therefore a marker in themselves). Keep in contact with one another with a shout of *cooee!* or some other loud yelp.

The deep dark forest isn't the only place where things can go wrong. Open meadows and river plains can be just as testing: markers can be far apart and hard to spot. There may be no set path, or maybe several. Riverbeds change course and bridges wash out. As you leave the bush and enter the open or approach the river, look for the next marker (often a large orange triangle) across the way. Be sure to re-enter the forest at the right point. The track might not continue where you thought it would. Look for the marker. Follow the marker. Look for the next marker and follow that one too.

> **TRACK MARKERS ARE OF NECESSITY** a discreet breed whose mistakes are sworn at and whose skill is acknowledged only by grunts and a boastful entry in the trampers' logbook that they 'did it' in only so-and-so hours. They should try it without a track.
>
> Mark Pickering, in *The Hills*, 1988

Watch where you're going

It's all very well having a map and compass, and following the markers, but your most powerful tool against getting lost is simple observation. Various things will tell you that you're on the right track: worn terrain underfoot, expected landmarks and geographical features (e.g. bluffs and streams). Look behind you as well as in front – if you have to retrace your steps, it's good to know what the track looks like from the opposite direction. Pay attention to your surroundings and tune in to the terrain.

> **LOOK FOR THE BEST FORDS IN A RIVER**, even if you are never likely to have to cross it; keep your eye open for good campsites ... Note the character of ridges and valleys, and especially note prominent objects so that you will recognise them again; taking it by and large, observation is the foundation stone of bushcraft.
>
> Arthur P. Harper, in *Moir's Guide North*, Geoff Spearpoint, 2005

GPS

The Global Positioning System, known as GPS, was originally designed for military purposes but is nowadays cheap and available to everyone. It works by triangulating your position using satellites orbiting the earth.

Most modern hand-held GPS receivers will give you an accurate three-dimensional fix, i.e. longitude, latitude and elevation. This is known as a waypoint. If you know the waypoint for a particular location (for example, a hut), you can input it into a GPS receiver, which will give you the bearing and distance to the location.

The main benefit of GPS is that it gives you your location almost instantaneously, normally to within plus or minus 100 metres (although accuracy can be affected by thick forest canopy or the walls of a deep gorge). If you're lost, or think you're lost, this information could save your life. However, these bearings and distances are 'as the crow flies'. You still need to plan your route, or you could find yourself walking off the end of a bluff. So, while it might seem that GPS is the answer to a walker's dreams (which they probably are, in the Sahara), they do have their limitations and are *not* a substitute for good navigation skills, a map and a compass.

If you decide to buy one, don't just rely on the sales assistant's advice – they may only tell you how good it is. There are numerous internet forums dedicated to recreational GPS use, some of which offer practical product reviews, hints and tips, downloadable maps and waypoints.

Blisters, bites and other annoyances

A little bit of suffering on the track is inevitable. As always, prevention is better than cure, but just in case, we offer the odd fix too.

Blisters

The best way to avoid blisters is to make sure your footwear fits correctly (see page 14). Even if it does you may still get the odd blister, especially if your boots are new or your feet are hot and wet. As soon as you feel your boots rubbing on a particular spot, stop and sort it out. (That means *right away*. Delay at your peril.) Check for wrinkly socks or a dodgy lace-up job. Tape over the spot with surgical tape or apply a dressing or plaster, being careful to avoid any creases.

If a minor blister has formed, cover it with a blister plaster or blister ring to keep pressure off the area. If your blister is bigger and has filled with fluid, pop it with a sterile needle, and drain out the fluid. Apply antiseptic cream and cover with a plaster, or gauze and tape.

Bites and stings

Sandflies are a pain in the ear, elbow, ankle and bum (if left uncovered). They are most active at dawn and dusk, and all day long in the Deep South. Mosquitoes, while less prevalent, can make a misery of a hot summer night. Your best protection against these pests is to cover up. This limits your exposure and thus avoids the need for lashings of repellent.

The active ingredient in most insect repellents is DEET. It may be effective but it's not very good for you, so use it sparingly or preferably not at all. Alternatives are readily available, or you can make your own.

Wasps are common in the New Zealand bush, particularly in beech forest in summer where they feed greedily on honeydew. They give a nasty sting and can be very dangerous for those with an allergy. If you see wasps flying about randomly, they are feeding and won't bother you a jot. But if you see lots of them and they look like they're on a mission – flying purposefully to and fro – you are about to stumble across a nest. Take a detour, delicately. If you do get stung, cool the affected area in a stream or river if possible. Be prepared for swelling, discomfort, and a good old itch as it comes right. Antihistamine cream or tablets will help.

NATURAL INSECT REPELLENT

Richard and Edwina from Okarito Nature Tours on the West Coast have kindly provided their recipe for DEET-free insect repellent. If it works there, it'll work anywhere!

WE MIX EIGHT PARTS carrier oil to one part citronella oil, but you could go up to a ratio of 5:1 – more than enough for most situations (even Fiordland!). We use sweet almond oil as a carrier, but you can use any oil that you are happy to apply to your skin. Of course there are times when the sandflies are swarming and nothing seems to work – typically in calm, humid weather just before it rains.

A good tip: citronella oil will also repel mosquitoes, but not as effectively as eucalyptus. If you are expecting a dual assault (sandflies and mozzies), add 10–15 per cent eucalyptus oil. It's a bit stinky, but that rarely bothers people when the bugs are biting.

One other tip: pure citronella oil bought from the pharmacy in small quantities is quite expensive. However, the cheap one-litre bottles of 'citronella oil' available at The Warehouse or hardware stores is for burning and NOT for putting on your skin.

All tramping party members should declare their allergies – particularly an allergy to wasp stings: an extreme reaction is known as anaphylactic shock, which is frighteningly swift and sometimes fatal. The common symptom of an obstructed airway will not aid the victim's efforts to tell you about it. Allergy-sufferers should not only tell you in advance of their affliction, but carry their medication and tell you where it's kept.

Sunburn

On summer tramping trips sunburn is almost impossible to avoid, and even the most careful covering up can still leave a patch of pink. It pays to avoid this. Around 300 New Zealanders die from skin cancer each year, the highest per capita rate in the world. This is partly because so many of us are lily white, but also because we're exposed to relatively high levels of UV via the hole in the ozone layer (we're not directly under it, but our ceiling is a bit patchy). In fact, our peak UV levels are about 40 per cent greater than those at comparable latitudes in Europe.

Being outdoors all day will dramatically increase your sunburn risk, especially when combined with wind and sea spray. The best way to avoid sunburn is to cover up. Take shelter in shade or slip on a shirt. Slap on a wide-brimmed hat: this is a *must*. Slop some sunscreen on to any exposed skin; SPF 30+ is good. (If you think this is starting to sound like a Sunsmart endorsement, you may be right.) If you do get burnt, keep the area covered. You could also apply soothing lotion such as After Sun, but this sounds like extra pack weight to me. Prevention is not only *better* but *lighter* than cure!

Heatstroke and dehydration

Heatstroke, or **heat exhaustion**, occurs when the body loses too much liquid, which is quite possible on arduous tramps in hot weather when you're sweating like mad. Sufferers will feel hot, bothered and headachy. Their heart rate may speed up and they may stop sweating. In extreme cases they may faint. It's fairly easily avoided though: don't tramp long and hard in the midday sun, and drink lots. If afflicted, seek shelter in the shade and cool your body – especially the head – with a wet cloth, and rehydrate slowly.

Dehydration is a common tramper's ailment. The telltale signs are headaches and infrequent, dark yellow pee, but dehydration can lead to other undesirable outcomes such as decreased blood pressure (with fainting a possibility), increased heart rate and delirium.

Constipation and dry skin are also symptomatic. All best avoided, we think you'll agree, so make sure you keep your fluids up, particularly in hot weather or when embarking on big climbs.

If you suspect you're suffering from dehydration:

- **Rehydrate slowly, taking small amounts of water often.** Purify the water if you're not sure about its cleanliness.
- Consider taking a dose of **rehydration salts** – such as Gastrolyte or Enerlyte – available in sachets from pharmacies.

Diarrhoea can cause or exacerbate dehydration, and for this you may consider **Imodium**. This medicine slows the rhythm of your digestion, allowing the body more time to absorb liquid and nutrients from food. However, use with caution: the toxins making you sick will not be purged as readily so your illness may in fact be prolonged.

Aches, pains and cramp

While aches and pains are inevitable, you *can* reduce your discomfort. Before you set off, **warm up with a few gentle stretches** – especially if you're about to pull on a heavy pack, and even more so early in the morning. **Start off slowly**, and ease into your stride. At the end of the day, stretch out – even if you're too tired to move. Just a few minutes will do: lie on your back and stretch your arms up over your head; scrunch up in a ball and roll from side to side; generally loll about. This will release some of the unwelcome lactic acid from your muscles. It really will help. A good old rub down with some Tiger Balm or Deep Heat will work wonders, too.

Cramp (an involuntary muscle contraction) is a distinct possibility in fatigued and slightly dehydrated bodies, and while not serious it can be extremely painful. It's most common in the calf, although anywhere in the legs is likely. If you get cramp, gently straighten out the offending limb and massage the muscle with slow, gentle strokes ... it will pass. Upping your intake of salt may help stave it off.

In desperate times, take desperate measures: painkillers are totally acceptable. Aspirin, paracetamol, Voltaren, any single malt – lightweight lifesavers every one ... always in moderation, of course.

Leaving no trace

Show respect for New Zealand's beautiful wild places by tidying up after yourself – *take only photos, leave nothing but footprints.*

The Environmental Care Code

Toitu te whenua – Leave the land undisturbed. This saying is at the heart of New Zealand's Environmental Care Code, the key points of which follow.

- **Protect plants and wildlife.** The areas you are visiting are home to many creatures, so be considerate of them. Our forests and birds are natural treasures, often unique and rare. Damaging or removing plants not only destroys part of the environment, it's often illegal. Many areas are fragile and may take years to recover. Wherever possible, find a way around alpine herb fields, moss beds, and coastal and wetland plants. Leave the dog at home (they are banned in many places, including national parks) and don't feed the birds – you're *not* doing them a favour.
- **Remove rubbish** (see page 72).
- **Use toilets provided** or **bury toilet waste.**
- **Keep streams and lakes clean.**
- **Take care with fires.** Use portable stoves for cooking. Build small, efficient fires using dead wood. Extinguish your fires completely (see pages 99–100).
- **Camp carefully.** Leave no trace of your visit (see page 99).
- **Keep to the track.** This is particularly important on high-use tracks. By keeping to the track, where one exists, you lessen the chance of damaging fragile plants. Resist the temptation to short cut corners – you can see the damage this does.

- **Consider others.** People visit the outdoors for many reasons. Be considerate: they have a right to enjoy themselves too.
- **Respect our cultural heritage.** Many places in New Zealand have special spiritual or historical significance. Some are sacred to Maori, while others have important European values. Recognise the spiritual or historical significance of these places and treat them with respect. Learning about places you visit will help you understand and respect the value they have for others.
- **Enjoy your visit!**

Rubbish removal

Rubbish is one of the biggest threats to our natural areas. Not only is it unpleasant, it encourages rats, mice, wasps and disease. It can also injure wildlife and human visitors. It is *not* acceptable to burn or bury rubbish or leave it for others to remove. Your rubbish is *your* responsibility:

- **Carry out what you carry in**, and if you come across someone else's rubbish, be a tidy Kiwi and carry that out too if you can (thank you, kind soul).
- **Minimise your waste**: buy products with less packaging, and leave excessive packaging at home.
- **Bury food scraps** in the same way as toilet waste (see opposite).
- Rinse your rubbish, compact it down, and **bag it up** well. At camp, make sure it's well guarded from critters.
- **Carry plenty of plastic bags** to double or triple bag it when it starts to get smelly.
- **Don't burn plastic** on the fire: it releases harmful dioxins into the atmosphere.
- When you get back to civilisation, **dispose of your rubbish carefully**.

Personal hygiene

One of the advantages of tramping in established recreational areas – national parks, forest parks and scenic reserves – is that they all offer at least a long drop loo (although many have compostable and even flush toilets nowadays). Most have a water supply too. This makes your ablutions easy and minimises your impact on the environment. However, the chances are that at some stage you'll need to poop in the bush and wash on the hop.

Human waste has already polluted our lakes and rivers – something you may learn first hand should you pick up the ghastly giardia (see page 91). To lessen the risk of contamination and protect our water quality, it's important that you carry out your ablutions in an environmentally friendly fashion:

- **Use the toilets** whenever you can.
- Where there's no toilet, **bury your toilet waste**. Choose a spot at least 50 metres from tracks, huts, campsites, picnic areas and any water sources. Dig a shallow hole – at least 15 centimetres deep – and when you're done, cover over all your waste and paper. A small trowel can be carried to assist with this duty, but a stick or your boot will also do the trick.
- When washing yourself or your utensils outside, draw the water and move well away from the source. Wash, then **drain the wastewater into the soil** (away from any water courses); this serves as a natural filter.
- Soaps and detergents are harmful to water life, so keep their use to a minimum and **use non-detergents and biodegradables** where you can. Remember: soapy water should be drained into the soil.

So, in summary: **don't wash up directly in the lake or stream.** Of course a swim is entirely okay – if you dare!

Before you go

Trip planning

Good planning will greatly enhance your tramping trip. Unlike most excursions, you can't pop to the shop to get what you forgot, or ring your mum to tell her you think you left the iron on. Once you've been on a few trips the planning stage will get easier, but until then **be methodical in your approach**. You'll be glad you did when the whole thing goes without a hitch.

Ask yourself some questions, and write yourself some notes. Use our checklists or make up your own. Aspects to think about are:

- **Is this tramp within your physical and technical limits?** Consider the terrain and your level of fitness – and the fitness of your walking partners. Make sure you can cover the distance at a comfortable pace within daylight hours (and what time does the sun set?). Do you possess the skills required, such as route finding and river crossing?
- **Who are you going with?** Choose your companions carefully. Ideally, they will be well matched to you in terms of fitness, motivation and expectations. If you're very new to tramping, it's best to go with people who are more experienced than you. At the very least, make sure your buddies are sensible, amiable and tolerant. A sense of humour won't go amiss either. Turn to page 86 for tips on how to avoid squabbles over rations.

> **IN THE HILLS YOU NOTICE QUICKLY** that friends snore, burp, fart, are stingy with their scroggin, skilful at getting the best possie in the tent and a dozen other minor irritations. You also see that they give generously of their chocolate, bring you a brew in bed, lend you gear, and help carry your gear when you are tired. You get to trust them.
>
> Mark Pickering, in *The Hills*, 1988

- **How long will it take?** For trampers, time is more important than distance – five kilometres walked on the flat may only take a couple of hours; on mountainous terrain it could take all day. Refer to your map or route guide, and estimate the time it will take to complete each leg. Walking times provided in books and pamphlets are useful, but only a guide. (DOC's walking times are pretty accurate and tend towards the conservative.)
- **Will you not only make it safely, but enjoy it as well?** Tramping isn't all about getting from A to B. A well-planned trip will allow you adequate rest stops and enough time to dawdle a bit: take in the views, watch a fantail flutter around you, or bathe in the river. Breathe. Relax. Contemplate.
- **How much food and water will you need?** Remember to allow for contingencies – it's better to have too much than not enough. Water requires particular consideration: you don't want to carry several (heavy) litres if there's a tap just round the corner. Check to see if – and where – there are drinkable water supplies on route. For more on food and water, see pages 80–91.
- **What equipment will you need?** Day-trippers should be able to sort this out in five minutes flat. Overnighters will have to think harder, and take more – especially campers. You're carrying your house on your back, after all. For more on equipment, see pages 24–47.

- **Do you need to book huts or campsites?** In peak season our national parks can be like Piccadilly Circus and you'll almost certainly have to book well in advance for the most popular tracks.
- **Are you crossing private land and do you need permission to do so?**
- **Do you need transport to or from the trail head?** Accessibility and transport services vary wildly from place to place, so definitely check in advance.
- **Have you told someone where you're going and when you'll be back?** Stating your intentions is an essential part of your safety plan – read on to learn more.

> To help avoid all manner of planning-related hiccups, see our **Trip planning checklist** and **Equipment checklist** at the end of this book.

Intentions

No one's going to come looking for you if they don't know you're missing. So follow the rule: **let someone know before you go.**

Leave details of your trip with a responsible person – it is their job to raise the alarm if you don't return on time. Day trippers and those on super-safe short tramps can probably just phone their mother.

But for back-country trips, you might want to consider filling in an **intentions form** too – this states where you're going and staying, who you're with, and when you're coming back. Forms can be downloaded from www.mountainsafety.org.nz. A good habit to adopt is to visit the local DOC visitor centre before you set off. You can lodge your intentions form here, and get last minute updates on weather and track conditions while you're at it.

Almost all huts have a **visitor's book** and you should always take the time to fill it in, even if you're just passing through. Not only does it provide a record of your visit and a chance to share with others your moments of natural exuberance (for example: 'Love the trees' or perhaps 'Rained all day. Hut full of school children'), but also your intended route beyond that point. This information is extremely valuable to searchers should you fail to return.

Please write down brief what you have seen,
Tell of the weather and the chase,
The luck you've had, and where you've been,
Then park the book safe in the case;
So that maybe when some man's son
Comes drifting in from off the spur,
He'll read what you have seen and done
When you were here in days that were.

Lester Masters, in *Backcountry Tales*, 1961

For extra insurance against being forgotten about, you could take with you one of several **communication devices** – a personal locator beacon, Mountain Radio Service transceiver, satellite phone or even just a cellphone (which may be out of range, but worth a try). For more information on these, turn to page 102.

When you return – fit and happy – at the end of your tramp, don't forget to let people know you got back safely.

Access and transport

Most of the places you visit – such as national and forest parks, scenic reserves and walkways – allow unrestricted access almost all of the time. However, you may occasionally need to cross **private land**. To do so you need to **obtain permission** from the landowner – without their permission you are liable to be trespassing. Not only can this be dangerous (because of raging bulls, electric fences, or just getting lost), it is ill-mannered and gives trampers a bad name.

Contact DOC to get the landowner's name, address or telephone number. Write or telephone them, outlining where and when you want to go. If permission is granted, remember to **be considerate of the landowner**:

- Park your car out of the way.
- Use stiles or gates where provided. Leave all gates as you find them.
- If you need to cross a fence, clamber carefully through the wires if you can, or cross at a post – don't pull at the wires this way and that.
- Try not to startle the livestock or trample any crops.
- When you get home, send the owner a letter of thanks.

If you're leaving your car at the trail head, be sure to leave it looking empty and boring. (A 1993 Nissan Bluebird is useful for this purpose, a brand new Subaru Legacy station wagon is not.) Thefts and vandalism do occur. Limit your chances of getting ripped off by locking anything remotely attractive – such as your new Phoenix Foundation CD – in the boot, out of sight. And when you return, be fully prepared to discover that a kea has eaten your windscreen wipers.

In some areas there may be a local **secure parking facility**. These are usually only a short walk or ride away and are well worth the modest expense. Use them if they're available – it will give you peace of mind *and* you'll be supporting the local economy.

If you don't have a car, getting yourself to and from the trail head requires some forward planning. **Public transport** will sometimes suffice, but more often than not the local bus will only take you so far. An extra five kilometres trudged on tarmac road can be tiring and tedious, not to mention straws and camels' backs.

Many tracks are serviced by **local transport operators** who run shuttles to and from the trail head at scheduled or pre-arranged times. The local visitor centre will have details. If no service exists, perhaps a kindly local could be persuaded to take you – this is not unheard of, especially in small-town New Zealand where everyone knows everyone and most people are good and kind. Failing this, consider a taxi. Shared between friends, the cost might not be that bad.

Some tracks are serviced by **small planes and boats** and this is a terrific way to start off or finish your tramp – often creating a circuit or saving a there-and-back trip. These journeys, while costly, will add texture and excitement to your experience. We once flew back over the Heaphy Track just a couple of hours after we finished it. Perfect blue skies and a stunning birdseye view of the track and terrain. We walked all that way? In just half an hour we were back where we started ... and ready to do it all again (but only after beer and a pie).

Food

Food is your fuel. Because you'll be active for most of the day you'll be burning many more calories than usual. So to keep you firing on all cylinders you'll need to eat more and eat well. But food has another role, too. It's full of cheer. The simplest of snacks – a square of chocolate, a single brazil nut or sliver of salami – will seem such a welcome reward. Food tastes better when you've earned it.

The trick to having enough tasty, nutritious food to keep you well and happy is **good planning**. Think carefully about what you need *before* you shop. There's nothing more frustrating than scratching around a dodgy dairy for last minute items when you're heading to the start of the track.

How long is your tramp and how many meals will you need? Is there any chance your trip will take longer than planned? If so, you'll need extra. The general rule is that it's better to have too much than too little, but don't overdo it. You'll be cross if you've carried a kilo of kumara that you unquestionably didn't require.

Choose your provisions well. Draw up a list of meals, and all the ingredients needed to make them. Consider options that are:

- high energy for weight
- nutritious
- as tasty and diverse as can be
- made of ingredients that won't go off
- quick and easy to prepare (less fuel, less equipment, less weight)
- uncrushable, compact and easy to carry

The tramper's pantry

The sort of food you take on your trip will depend on how long you'll be away. For one or two day trips you can bring in a bottle of grog and a ten-ounce steak. But for longer trips, the bulk of your food should be dried. (Buy it ready dried, or if you're particularly enterprising you can buy a dehydrator – your local health food store may be able to get one for you.) Your dry supplies should be supplemented with carefully chosen fresh items, ranked and then eaten according to perishability. If it won't keep long, eat it first.

Provisions should be chosen with nutrition in mind. You need carbohydrates and plenty of them; in fact they should constitute 60–70 per cent of your supplies. The other 30–40 per cent should be split between proteins and fats.

The tramper's pantry is likely to contain items from each of the following groups:

- **Ready meals** (e.g. Continental Pasta & Sauce, Rice Risotto, Back Country Cuisine, Cup-a-Soup, Two-minute Noodles) – these will probably form the basis of your main meals. They vary greatly in quality; some are of limited nutritional value while others taste like reconstituted cardboard. Vegetables, sauces and spices, etc., can be added to bolster and add interest (see page 87).
- **Plain pasta, noodles** and **rice** – go for quick cooking varieties: it will save you time and fuel. If you take these, you'll need something to go with them (e.g. vegetable, sausage, sauce or stock cube).
- **Cured meats** – salami, chorizo and suchlike will stay good all week, while ham and bacon can come along too but need to be eaten sooner.
- **Tinned meats** and **fish** – well worth the weight. Look for tuna in the plastic pouch – perfect for this purpose.
- **Cheese** – a tasty source of protein: hard cheeses (e.g. cheddar or parmesan) will last longer and take the knocks.

- **Nuts** – an excellent source of energy and the tramper's best friend. Any shelled nut will do. See scroggin recipe on page 85.
- **Fruit** – dried fruit is compact, light and tasty, so that's your pick. Fresh fruit is heavy, but if you are prepared to carry it, look for durable fruits such as apples and oranges. Bananas much prefer to stay at home, unless they're dried and chipped.
- **Vegetables** – as with fruit, look for durable or dried vegetables. Red peppers are robust, as are carrots and beans. Potato flakes, dried peas, carrots and beans are a good option too, as are dried mushrooms.
- **Bread** – there a couple of things to consider here. One is the squash factor; some loaves will cave in or crumble under pressure, so look for something robust and unsliced. Good white options are pita bread or soft tortillas. And as bread may be one of your major sources of carbohydrate, a slow-burning loaf is your best bet – look for wholemeal breads with grain and seed. **Crackers** are good too, but we're talking hardy buggers, not flaky water crackers.
- **Cereals** – go for wholesome options: porridge oats, muesli and Weetbix, for example.
- **Milk** – we think you'd be pretty mad to carry fresh milk or even UHT. Powdered milk is a more than adequate substitute; whole milk powder is best, with more calories and better flavour.
- **Spreads** and **oils** – peanut butter is a good option, being highly calorific and packed with protein. Vegemite (or, heaven forbid, Marmite) is rich, tasty and offers a boost of vitamins and minerals. Hummus, pesto and suchlike will last several days and break up the boredom of cheese. Butter and margarine are fine in cooler conditions, but take only what you need. Butter can be used for cooking too, or take a little oil instead. Jam, marmalade and honey offer a welcome, quick-burning sugar rush. Look for products in lightweight squeezy tubes or small plastic jars – or decant into something similar.

- **Teas, coffee, cocoa** and **sugar** – you might also like powdered fruit drink sachets such as Raro, an instant sugar hit when you need it.
- **Herbs, spices** and **sauces** – these lightweight condiments will transform your food. Salt, pepper, dried herbs, spices and pastes, mustards, chutneys and rich sauces: take only what you need, decanted into plastic. See our tips for gourmet tramping on page 87.
- **Sweets** and **treats** – it's a good idea to keep plenty of quick-release energy on hand. Biscuits (gingernuts and Anzacs are great), muesli bars, boiled sweets, toffees and chocolate are a good pick me up, mentally and physically. And scroggin, the eponymous wonder food, should always be at hand of course!

> **SIMPLE STRONG FLAVOURS** seem to work better than complex mushes. Bacon and rice, salami and noodles, cheese and macaroni, these have all been tried and tested through thousands of stomachs. Curry powder can cover up many a cooking disaster, and so can hunger. If the result is looking unfortunate, keep them waiting. The food will not stay in the region of their taste buds long enough for them to pass judgement.
>
> Mark Pickering, in *The Hills*, 1988

Menu planning

Food plays such an important part in your trip that it's well worth getting out your pen and paper and planning all your meals in advance. Decide what you want to eat, then list all the ingredients and the quantities required. This will also help you estimate your cooking fuel requirements. Remember, some meals require more fuel than others – so keep fuel demands in mind, particularly for long trips.

What it pays to consider here is that beyond breakfast and before dinner, you are on the move. You will neither want to nor be able to enjoy a big, hot, sit-down lunch. Rather, you'll want to snack all day – a handful of scroggin here, a biscuit there, a slab of bread and cheese around midday. This makes sense. Don't eat by the clock: eat as your body demands it. Keep refuelling – but be careful to stick to your rations.

Below, we give you some menu suggestions. You'll have your own preferences, of course, and your own limits of what you're prepared to carry.

Breakfast

- porridge, muesli or other cereal with dried fruit, apples, etc., served with milk (reconstituted from powder)
- bread and spreads
- bacon sandwich (our pick)
- tea, coffee or fruit drink

Lunch

- bread, crackers
- cured meat, tinned fish, cheese
- fresh fruit or vegetables (e.g., apples or carrots)
- biscuits
- scroggin
- tea, coffee or fruit drink

Dinner

- pasta with salami and cheese
- risotto with tomato, tuna and herbs
- noodles with dried vegetables and oriental spices
- mashed potato (flakes) with sausage and vegetables
- soup with bread, and fruit to follow
- ready-made backpacker meal

Snacks

- scroggin
- muesli bars
- biscuits and crackers
- dried fruit
- boiled sweets

DON'T FORGET YOUR SCROGGIN!

Scroggin – the New Zealand name for the high-energy snack that some boring old nations call trail mix – is a ubiquitous mixture of dried fruits, nuts and other nibbles. You can read about its origins at the front of this book.

Choose your favourite ingredients (as long as it's not *all* chocolate), and mix them up in a plastic bag or two. Plan to have enough for the whole trip – it really will keep you going.

We reckon an average tramper will need around 150 grams of scroggin on a full day's tramp (in addition to breakfast, lunch and dinner). A typical batch would consist of several of the following things:

- **nuts**, roasted or raw: peanuts, almonds, brazils, macadamias, coconut ...
- **dried fruits**: raisins, apricots, cranberries, dates, banana chips ...
- **chocolate**: coated raisins, dark squares, jaffas ...
- **seeds**: pumpkin, sunflower, sesame, pine kernels ...
- **boiled sweets**: barley sugars, hard toffees, mints ...

You can of course add anything you like but remember to aim for high energy, variety and enjoyment.

GROUP MENU PLANNING

Poorly planned menus or insufficient quantities can cause niggles and gripes. In the interests of promoting group harmony we present here some useful group menu-planning advice from seasoned tramper, Shaun Barnett.

FOR GROUP TRIPS, a tried and true method I have used (let's say four people on a four night trip) is that each individual organises their own breakfasts, lunches, drinks and snacks and **one** of the evening meals. This has several advantages:

- Everyone gets to choose food that suits them best during the day (vegetarians, vegans, fuss-pots and intolerants can cause complications in a co-ordinated menu scenario).
- Each person is responsible for rationing (and carrying) their own supplies – everyone is free to be as greedy or minimalist as they like.
- Evening meals have more variety – everyone is bound to come up with something different to share.
- It takes the organisational load off any one person, and means that everyone carries more or less the same load to the trail head (this is particularly important if you're flying in and have a weight restriction on your baggage).

The gourmet tramper

A daily diet of two-minute noodles is as dull as dishwater and we recommend you avoid this as best you can. Your options are restricted by weight and cooking facilities, so there will invariably be some deprivation, but this is good for you. You'll rediscover the joys of simple food and the ancient art of the one-pot wonder. You'll be forced to be a bit creative. Use your noodle and make tramping food fun!

Here's our advice for eating well and enjoying it even when you're in the middle of nowhere:

- **Fresh meat and vegetables** can be taken if used in the first one or two days.
- Decant small quantities of tasty **condiments** into leak-proof plastic bottles: chutneys, pickles, mustard, sauces and pastes.
- Make up your own **herb and spice mixes** to give your boring boil-ups a boost: Italian herbs (oregano, rosemary, thyme), Indian spice mix (curry powder, garam masala, chilli flakes), etc.
- **Freshly ground coffee** will give you a real rev-up in the mornings. No filter required; just allow the grounds to settle to the bottom of the billy and pour out gently. Chocolate-covered coffee beans may also float your boat.
- **A little nip of whisky** or such will do you no end of good! Decant into a plastic bottle and eke out for extended enjoyment (if you are capable of such self-restraint – we aren't).
- **Fishing** or **hunting** can reward you with some of New Zealand's finest kai, but be sure you have the correct licence or permit, and know your limits.

Remember: if you're only going bush for a night or two, and particularly if you're staying in a hut, you can take almost anything you like. While honeymooning in Aspiring Hut (with ten other trampers

– romantic, eh?), we whipped up a dinner of fillet steak with pepper sauce, mashed potato and sautéed garlic mushrooms. (Actually, fantastic new husband whipped it up while lazy wife lolled about. Start as you mean to go on.) We washed it down with a Central Otago pinot noir. Sublime. You should have seen the look on the faces of our fellow hutters, their noses all a-twitch ...

Rations and packaging

Once you've gathered your food supplies, review and sort them before packing. This is quite important: not only can you check that you've got everything you need, you can also ditch excess items and packaging.

Sort your food into rations and recalculate your quantities. If you've got too much of certain things (e.g. a whole bag of sugar), portion off what you need and leave the rest behind. Discard any unnecessary packaging (being careful to keep any important cooking instructions) and – where sensible – **repackage the food** into sealable plastic bags or lightweight plastic containers. Escapable items such as milk powder or sugar should be double-bagged; use small containers for sauces, chutneys and sufficient quantities of spreads. Your food rations are now as light as they can be, and the good news is they'll only get lighter as you go along.

Now, **sort the items** into logical bunches and pack into larger plastic bags or stuff sacks. This not only insures against spillage, it helps you find what you want when you need it, and assists in dividing the load between friends.

When loading food into your pack, remember to keep lunches, scroggin and other snack foods near the top of your pack.

Watch for others who seek to eat your food. Mice are not infrequent visitors in the night. Pack up food well and if possible, store it out of reach. And **please don't feed the wildlife.**

Water

Water is an essential part of the tramper's trip. You need it to prepare your meals, wash your dishes, and keep yourself clean. Most importantly though, you need it for drinking. With all that physical activity, you'll need to drink a lot more water than usual – a couple of cupfuls an hour is a good ballpark figure.

For day trips, fill up a big bottle at home. For overnight tramps, you'll have to be a bit more clever. Carrying a 5-litre bottle of spring water is unnecessary, ridiculous in fact. Better to **plan ahead**: where are the water sources and are they fit to drink? Your map or route guide will indicate available sources, whether it's a tap at the toilets or hut, or a natural watercourse (i.e. a river or stream).

At toilets and huts, you may see a sign such as 'Water must be boiled for a least three minutes before drinking.' That is your cue to do so. In the absence of official advice, it's up to you to decide whether to drink it untreated or not. The question we generally ask ourselves is, where is this water coming from? Is there any chance it could be contaminated? If you are unsure of the quality of the water, treat it.

A FRIEND TOLD ME A STORY about the night she was sent to fetch water supplies for her tramping party.

Arriving at bush camp late in the evening, after dark, she set off down to the creek to fill up the billy for the evening meal. Despite the dark, there was nothing to the task: the creek was easily accessible and flowing nicely, and she quickly returned with sufficient quantities which were duly consumed.

In the morning, she returned to the same spot to fetch water for breakfast. And what did she discover? A festering sheep's carcass – obviously there for quite some time – trapped by a rock just a few metres upstream.

Sarah Bennett

MAKING WATER FIT TO DRINK

If your tramping trip requires you to drink the water along the way, and you're not sure of its purity, be prepared to treat it. There are several methods of doing this, but note that only filtering will actually remove any suspended matter (otherwise known as 'greeblies'):

- **Boiling** – three minutes on a rolling boil is easily sufficient. This is the most effective way of making water safe to drink, although it requires being stationary to fire up the camp-stove.
- **Chemical treatment** – typically iodine or chlorine. These take some time to take effect, sometimes 20–30 minutes, so you'll have to wait that long before you can drink it.
- **Filtering** – water filters can also be purchased from outdoor stores. They are effective at removing most contaminants; they are, of course, extra equipment to carry.

Be aware that no amount of boiling, treating or filtering will remove some chemical toxins from water. If you even remotely suspect that a water source could be contaminated by pesticides from farmland, or waste from an industrial site (what lies upstream?), don't even think about drinking it.

As many of New Zealand's lakes and rivers are not fit for drinking, you should never assume they are, even if the water looks crystal clear and fresh. That said, drinking fresh cool water straight from the source is one of tramping's great pleasures, so if you're confident it's safe then do it.

The ugly bug you are most likely to swallow is **giardia**. Fairly widespread in New Zealand, this troublesome parasite is spread mainly via poorly disposed toilet waste. It can survive long periods in cold water – including those delicious-looking lakes, rivers and streams.

Giardia infects the intestines of humans, as well as those of cattle, possums and other animals. If you pick it up, expect chronic diarrhoea, nausea, stomach cramps, dehydration, fatigue, headaches and weight loss. Symptoms will most likely emerge 5–7 days after infection, and while the illness is most acutely felt for only a few days, the affected person may remain infected for months afterwards if untreated.

Sound pretty dreadful? If there is *any* chance of giardia in the water, treat it before you drink it. And to help protect others from infection, remember to toilet thoughtfully and practise the best possible camp hygiene (see pages 71–73).

If you are striken by severe diarrhoea, or simply don't drink enough water, you may become dehydrated. For tips on dealing with this condition, see pages 69–70.

Shelter

There are generally two bedtime options for the overnight tramper – huts and camping. Assuming that both options are open to you (something to assess early on in your planning stage as this will affect your gear selection), there are distinct advantages and disadvantages to each option.

Huts

PROS

- It's dry, and relatively comfortable.
- You don't have to carry (or even own) a tent or a sleeping mat, so your pack is lighter.
- In a small number of huts, gas stoves are provided – so that will also save you weight (although you still need to carry other cooking gear, i.e. your pots and pans).
- There may be a fireplace, or pot-belly stove for warming bodies and drying wet boots. However, do not assume that fuel will always be available.
- You will always be near to a toilet, even if it's a long drop. You'll almost certainly have running water, too.
- You meet interesting people.

CONS

- Lack of privacy.
- You are forced into close quarters with random folk, who are sometimes loud, annoying, smelly, or worse ... snorers.

- As a communal environment, you will be forced into being more considerate and tolerant than usual. This can be hard when it comes to packing crinkly food bags at 6 a.m.
- They can be a bit grubby, and sometimes there are mice – and spiders.
- They are more expensive than camping (which is often free), although they're still pretty darn cheap.
- You sometimes need to book in advance (and almost definitely on Great Walks).

DOC huts

If you haven't stayed in a DOC hut before, you're missing out: they're fantastic in so many ways. There are a staggering number of them – around 1000 in fact, of which two-thirds are in the South Island. Not only have they been built in some of our most spectacular and out-of-the-way places, but every one is different and most have a story to tell. And yet they're easy to find and cheap to stay in. Some can be booked via DOC's website (www.doc.govt.nz) or local visitor centres.

The huts vary in quality, facilities, popularity and price: all to be considered before you set off, as this will affect the gear you need to carry (including cash – credit cards and eftpos are *not* available). Services and facilities change from time to time, and from season to season, so always check with DOC before you venture out.

You'll need to book for many of the Great Walk huts (and campsites), but generally not for serviced or standard huts. In the busy season, though, the huts may be full. It always pays to check with DOC before you set out to see how busy they are. If there is a chance you will not secure a bunk, take a sleeping mat as backup (you can sleep on the floor), or take camping gear.

Backcountry Hut Passes and **Hut fees** can be paid for at DOC visitor centres. Basic huts are free to use, while fees for other huts vary according to the hut grading.

DOC HUT GRADINGS

Great Walk huts
Offer mattresses, water supply, hand-washing, toilets and heating facilities. Most – but not all – have cooking facilities with fuel, but no cooking utensils. Some have solar lighting. A warden is usually in residence.

Serviced huts
Bunks or sleeping platforms with mattresses, water supply, heating (and fuel during the peak season), toilet and hand-washing facilities. Some have cooking facilities and a warden in residence. Serviced alpine huts have the same facilities except heating.

Standard huts
Standard huts have bunks or sleeping platforms with mattresses, a toilet and water supply. Wood-burning heaters are provided at most huts below the bushline (fuel is collected by hut users).

Basic huts & bivvies
Very basic shelter with limited facilities.

Note: Most DOC huts are in the basic and standard categories.

Thinking of bringing the **dog**? Dogs are not allowed in the national parks, but they are allowed in some other DOC areas, unless indicated. Dogs are not allowed in or under the huts – keep them away. And please don't take your dog into areas where there are native flightless birds such as kiwi or weka.

Lodges, cabins and cottages

In addition to the hut network, DOC also manages more upmarket accommodation in scenic settings nationwide. They are basic, but comfortable, and easily accessible by car, boat or short walk. While not five-star by any stretch, they're ideal for learner trampers, families, school and other groups, offering more room to move, electricity, and sometimes a hot shower. All require booking in advance.

Other back-country huts

In addition to DOC huts, there are a large number of other huts dotted around the country, mostly owned by local tramping, alpine and mountaineering clubs. Some are available to the general public; check with your local club for details. There are also privately-owned huts, particularly on South Island high-country pastoral leases. Only use these if you have permission or in an emergency.

> **JUST AS YOU'RE ABOUT TO DRIFT OFF** to sleep, a snorer starts. At first it's just a wheezy kind of whistle, but then, in a frighteningly abrupt snort, the snorer really gets going. Long vibrating intakes of breath are followed by whooshing expulsions. You can hear others are awake now, all tossing and rustling in their sleeping bags. Some let out long, audible sighs of discontent. Others mutter under their breath 'For God's sake ...'
>
> The answer lies with anti-snore devices. Earplugs can be effective against minor offenders, but some will need firmer measures. Have a few missiles at the ready. Soft items should be thrown first (a pair of socks), with increasingly heavier and harder items saved till later (boots). A tin of pineapple is ideal, and can be so effective as to render the snorer too frightened for attempts at further sleep, which is ultimately your goal.
>
> Shaun Barnett, in 'Some huts do have 'em',
> *Wilderness*, May 2000

HUT ETIQUETTE

Within New Zealand tramping culture there are some simple, but cherished traditions of hut etiquette. You won't find these written down anywhere, but happily they are straightforward, and simply call for basic consideration and friendliness.

Without a doubt, a great attitude to take into the back country is to regard it as a place where the shared experience and communal living give you an opportunity to leave behind some of the insularity that commonly goes with modern urban living.

Older trampers often bemoan the change in hut culture over the last 30 odd years in New Zealand. Some of this is inevitable, as huts, especially on the Great Walks, have got far bigger and busier, and therefore more impersonal. But nonetheless, there are still plenty of things you can do to make the experience more enjoyable for you and your fellow trampers.

Here are some simple ways of behaving that can really impact on sharing a hut:

- **Be friendly to your fellow trampers.** We're not suggesting that everyone needs to be your best friend, but it is far nicer to share a communal space when there is some personal warmth about.
- **Be welcoming of any other trampers that arrive after you.** After all, you don't actually own the hut, and there is nothing worse than arriving at a hut to be greeted by cool, unfriendly people. One of the worst sins though is to be unwelcoming to trampers if the hut is full and there are no bunks left. Traditionally

in this situation, old-style trampers would always squeeze up by 'top and tailing' and fitting two people to a bunk. If you are not comfortable with this, then at the very least clear some floor space and welcome people in. They will often have no choice but to use the hut. As well, it is good to remember that the time will come when you will arrive at a hut in the pouring rain at nightfall, only to find it full, so treat others as you would like to be treated yourself.

- **Leave wet coats and wet, muddy boots outside** in the porch or on the veranda (except in kea country), and try to keep the hut floor as dry as possible.
- **If you use any firewood replace it with dry wood,** though better still, leave more than you used. And if you can find some dry twigs that would be good for starting a fire, it is always a nice gesture to set these aside somewhere obvious. There is nothing like arriving at a cold empty hut and finding that some kind soul has laid out the kindling for you!
- **Be generous when you can.** If you have spare hot water, offer it around, and if you have excess food, offer that around – it will be really appreciated.
- **Keep your noise down,** especially when anyone is sleeping.
- When you go, **leave the hut tidier than you found it.**
- Always, always **make sure the door is securely shut** when you leave.

Robbie Burton

Camping

PROS

- You have greater freedom in choosing where to stop for the night.
- Peace and quiet. Go to bed and get up when you like, without being disturbed by bag-crinklers and snorers.
- Privacy ... for those special moments.
- You are truly amongst the elements – from the rain on the fly to the night sky.

CONS

- You have to carry the tent – an extra 2–3 kilos.
- Weather. It's all very well having a super-dooper waterproof tent, but at some stage you've got to venture out of it. Think about cooking and nipping to the loo.
- Lack of facilities.
- Lack of headroom. Expect to spend your evenings of Travel Scrabble lying down, propped up on an elbow.

The great advantage of camping over hutting is that you can just about sleep where you like: you can really be alone in the wilderness. Oh, sweet bliss. However, camping has its challenges – mostly centred around extra pack weight and the weather, but it need not be uncomfortable. With the right gear and practice, it can be entirely pleasurable in the most unlikely conditions.

Campsites can pretty much be split into two groups – designated campsites (obligatory on the Great Walks) and freedom camping, which is to say that you can camp almost anywhere you like.

Where possible, camp at **designated campsites**. They are there to make your life easier and limit your impact on the environment. Often located near to huts and almost always situated in optimal spots – flat, elevated, and close to a stream or lake for bathing – they usually have a water source and a loo. Some even provide a shelter; priceless in the rain for cooking, packing up, and a bit of a social.

If it's **freedom camping** you're after, the first thing to do is check with DOC or the local council that it is permitted, and follow any rules and regulations they lay down. As for the actual location, we suggest you start assessing your options well before dark. It's not always easy to find a good spot, but remember:

- Try to camp at least 100 metres from the track.
- Look for level ground, shelter and a water source.
- Keep your camp clean and carry all your rubbish out with you.
- Use your camp stove if possible; keep campfires minimal and legal (see below for more on fire safety).

The bottom line is **leave no trace of your visit.** Turn to page 71 for a few more tips on this subject.

Lighting fires

A trip in the great outdoors often allows an opportunity to light a small fire for cooking or warmth, one of life's primeval and practical pleasures.

There's some who long for scent of gums,
Some for the scent of oak,
While others yearn to smell once more,
Scent of manuka smoke.
That scent of hills and mountain vales,
Which holds the memory
Of winding tracks and lonely shacks
And bush fraternity.

Lester Masters, in *Backcountry Tales*, 1961

However, fires have environmental consequences, which can sometimes be devastating. For a starter, fires need wood. Those large branches or logs you're burning are a source of food and shelter for many forest insects and plants. But of course this isn't the worst that can happen.

Uncontrolled fires are one of the greatest threats to our natural environment, and the awful effects of it are obvious. Would you want to be responsible for the mass destruction of a beautiful forest? (And then liable for the cost of the fire-fighting? Fines have run up to $100,000!)

Fire safety is of vital importance:

- Be aware of **fire bans** and **higher fire risk** during summer months. You may need a permit for your fire. DOC or the local council can tell you whether a ban is in place. These rules exist to protect us all, so adhere to them.
- **Be careful with camp stoves**: operate them at least 2 metres away from dry vegetation.
- If you have to light a campfire, keep it small and use only **dead wood**. Select wood from riverbeds or areas where it is plentiful.
- **Use existing fireplaces if possible,** or build your fire in a sheltered spot away from dry vegetation and hanging branches. Ensure you have ready access to a water source to douse it.
- Make sure the fire is **completely extinguished** by soaking it with water or covering it with sand or soil. Check that the ashes are cold. Dismantle the fire site, and scatter unburnt wood before leaving the area.
- **Never leave fires unattended.**

PADDY'S POEM

In my little shack in the supplejack
at the foot of the hill on Holdsworth Track
where the tramper toils, where the billy boils
and the pig and the deer walk free
and the sunset gleams on mountain streams
as they wander to the sea
and when darkness falls and the morepork calls
as he flits from tree to tree
it's lonely I know, as the cold wind blows
but it's home sweet home to me.
In my little shack in the supplejack
where someday my soul be free
to roam up high on the mountain top
where the moon comes up so clear
and the snow capped mountains hem you in
with a silence you can almost hear
when high above, the call of love
from a lonely stag you hear
and the stars come out, and they dance about
and the mountains seem so near
and the sun comes up from behind the hill
and the birds all seem to cheer.

Anonymous, from the Holdsworth Lodge hut book

Survival skills

If you are well prepared and sensible, the chances are that you will never get lost or need rescuing. However, sometimes a change in circumstances is unforeseen – extreme weather shifts, accidents or injuries can happen – and even the most experienced tramper can get into trouble.

If this happens to you, the decisions that follow can mean the difference between life and death. A responsible tramper should know how to handle the most likely scenarios.

Prevention is always better than cure, of course, and being well prepared is definitely the best way to avoid life-threatening situations. Your local tramping club and the Mountain Safety Council offer useful courses such as bushcraft, first aid, river crossings and survival skills, and you are well advised to consider taking one or two of these. You can find their details under **Useful Contacts** at the end of this book.

Communication devices

On the track, you may need to communicate with the outside world – to obtain the latest weather information, update your intentions, or raise the alarm in an emergency. For low-risk tramping trips, a properly lodged intentions form and a cellphone for backup will probably suffice. However, if you're embarking on a more challenging trip or tramping alone, a specialised communication device should be considered.

Cellphone

While you occasionally hear stories of cellphones saving people's lives, a clear signal cannot be guaranteed in many of our tramping areas – so don't count on this as a method of communication. That said, it is well worth throwing your phone in your pack, fully charged; even low or intermittent reception can be sufficient to squeeze out a text message, especially if you climb a nearby hill.

Satellite Phone

Similar to a cellphone in size and weight, this phone receives coverage in any location worldwide provided it has a clear view of a satellite. The signal may be reduced in deep gorges or dense bush. These phones are expensive to buy and operate; they can, however, be hired from specialist communications and equipment suppliers.

Mountain Radio Service

The Mountain Radio Service (MRS) operates nationwide communication centres and hires out high-frequency transceivers and aerials (sometimes known as a 'field set') for those going on more remote and challenging trips. The MRS offers one of the most reliable forms of back-country communication; the field sets work just about anywhere, while the volunteers at the communication centres are there specifically to look out for you. Note though, this is not a substitute for declaring your intentions; the MRS will not instigate a search if they don't hear from you. However, you can use a field set to call for help in an emergency.

Users set up daily scheduled contact times (known as 'scheds') during which weather, location and intentions information is exchanged. Outside of sched times, any emergency call you transmit may well be picked up by another service, or radio operator listening in. Note that some services are restricted according to location and time of year. Contact details for the MRS are listed in the **Useful Contacts** section.

DOC hut warden radios

DOC hut wardens will have a radio for management purposes and will happily relay the latest weather forecast and track conditions. The radio can of course be used in an emergency. However, don't count on them as a life-saver as they are few and far between.

Emergency locator beacons (ELB)

Emitting a radio signal on an international distress frequency, an ELB should only be activated in life-threatening situations. Your location is relayed to the Rescue Coordination Centre via satellite or aircraft. Can be purchased or hired from outdoor equipment shops.

Emergency plan

So, what will you do if you get lost, injured, stranded by a flooded river or fail to reach your hut by dark? If in any of these scenarios you find yourself without water, shelter, warmth, food or the will to survive, you may be facing a potentially life-threatening situation. It is important that everyone in your group knows what to do.

Stop, stay calm and plan

- **Assess your circumstances.** If you're lost, you may be able to retrace your steps. Try to pinpoint your location on your map.
- **Evaluate your options.** Consider the resources you have and to what degree will they help you cope.
- **Seek help.** Keep an eye out for other trampers – *never* be afraid to ask help from others.

> **BUT WHAT ABOUT A PARTY** which has gone blindly into difficult country with no sense of direction or power of observation? What should they do? I should say the first thing would be to sit down and have a smoke.
>
> Federated Mountain Clubs,
> 'Safety in the Mountains', 1949

Keep warm

- Find or make a **shelter** to protect you from the elements. Select a safe site; one that won't flood, isn't exposed to rock falls, and is below the bushline; under fallen trees or natural overhangs is a good option.
- Put on additional **dry clothing.**
- Make a **fire,** if possible. See page 106 for tips on lighting a fire in the rain.
- Use a sleeping bag, mat, survival bag/emergency blanket or vegetation to **insulate yourself** from the damp, cold ground. Another option is to climb into your pack.
- **Cover yourself** with dry vegetation, such as fern fronds or tussock, for additional insulation.

Drink plenty of water and ration your food

While it is not desirable to go without food, you can survive for days without it, so long as you stay warm, rest and drink plenty of water (as long as you have plenty of reserves to hand – otherwise, ration that too).

Conserve your energy

If you need to move around or want to explore your options, make all your decisions good ones. Use your energy efficiently: you may need to harness everything available for one big push to safety, or simply to stay alive until help comes.

Be determined to survive

It is not unusual to feel fearful but you must tell yourself that you will survive. Dig down deep for courage and every ounce of determination you can muster.

LIGHTING FIRES FOR SURVIVAL

Learning how to light a fire in all conditions, including in the rain, is a great skill to learn, and can make a real difference in a survival situation, where warmth, and the ability to dry wet clothes really matters.

The only way to get good at firelighting is to practise, but it is a very rewarding thing to do. The most useful thing to learn is how to select dry, seasoned wood, and how to avoid rotten wood, which will never burn – using rotten wood is the most common mistake that inexperienced firelighters make. If you can find and recognise seasoned wood, even if it is damp, you can always light a fire and keep it going.

Often such wood is standing, part of a dead tree or branch, and has not yet started to rot. But often the most reliable wood to be found in the hills is actually driftwood, found in surprising abundance if you look carefully in riverbeds and other watercourses.

When you start a fire, have all the wood you need to get it going, ready and waiting before you begin, and then start small, and build it up carefully and steadily. This is an exercise in patience. Use a billy lid as a fan, or blow on the base of the fire to get the flame to catch if necessary.

A great thing to use as a firelighter is the stub of a candle. Set that at the bottom of your prospective fire, light it and gradually cover with very small twigs.

Always carry a lighter, or a box of matches wrapped in plastic for an emergency.

A TRÈS BON FIRE

We were trying to get from the East Matukituki over Rabbit Pass into the Wilkin River, but persistent nor'west rain had kept us pinned down in the cirque below the pass. On the second night, during a spectacular electrical storm, the heavens opened and the mountainsides all around us were transformed into one huge sheet of water. Despite the fact that we were camped on a slope, well away from any water-course, by midnight there were centimetres of water flowing under the tent, as well as through it, and it was as if we were sleeping on a particularly objectionable, porous waterbed.

The night was long, cold and miserable, and virtually everything we had, including what little food we had left, got completely soaked.

At dawn we knew that we desperately needed warmth, so after a couple of hairy river crossings we managed to get downstream to the bush at Ruth Flat. Here we coaxed a small fire into life, which we carefully, slowly built until we were feeding a serious bonfire with small logs that we were dragging off the flat in a frenzy of activity. The resulting conflagration allowed us, over the course of that drizzly afternoon, to dry our sleeping bags and clothes to a habitable state, and I shall never forget the indescribable pleasure of slipping into a dry sleeping bag as night fell, snug and warm under the shelter of the beech trees, and untroubled by the light patter of rain on the tent.

If ever I was grateful for the sustenance of fire, this was the time.

Robbie Burton

Seeking help and getting found

If one of your group is injured or goes missing, you may need to seek help from the outside world. If you're carrying an MRS transceiver, ELB, satellite phone or functioning cellphone, then these should be employed. However, getting assistance may not be quite that easy. You may need to send someone – and if possible, two people – out with a message. These people should be fit, reliable and have a clear idea of their mission. Any departing messengers should observe and mark their route out carefully so the stranded party can easily be found again (*à la* Hansel and Gretel).

However you get your distress message out – via a communication device or on foot – make sure you communicate the vital details of your predicament:

- what has happened, when and where
- details of the missing person/people and other group members
- details of injuries/illness
- resources currently on hand: clothing, food, equipment and experience
- action taken and immediate plans – how were things when you left?

The injured party or group should now keep together and wait for rescue – **always stay put unless you are sure you can find your way out**. However, if you need to move to a safer site, or if changing circumstances allow you to make your way to safety, make sure that your searchers can follow you. Leave notes, cairns, tree-blazes or such, indicating the route you have taken.

While waiting for rescue, make your location visible to air and ground rescue teams:

- if safe to do so, move your group to an open area nearby
- drape brightly coloured clothing or equipment in view
- light a smoky fire with green leaves
- if you see your rescuers, wave your arms or jump up and down to attract attention
- blow a whistle
- flash a mirror

If you are lost or injured **on your own,** most of these still apply. However, you will need to make all the decisions yourself. Evaluate your situation carefully and weigh up the dangers and benefits of either seeking out help or waiting for the rescue services to find you. Above all, remember to stay calm and **never give up**.

HOW IT CAN ALL GO WRONG

This true story tells of a tramper who tried to complete the challenging Southern Crossing of the Tararuas – alone, poorly equipped, and in bad weather. Thanks to our anonymous survivor for sharing it, and paramedic Johnny Mulheron for his summary.

I was already tired from a full-on New Year. I stayed first in Field Hut, then went up in good weather to Kime. The forecast had said the weather would stay good, however, the wind and rain started in the night. I slept badly. An experienced tramper had come over from Alpha, and when he heard my plans to go over the top he advised me against it.

However, I set off regardless – after all, it wasn't too bad at the hut. But by the time I got up on the tops it was so windy I could only move by hanging on to rocks. I'd left my boots at home because they were worn out, and I only had my old running shoes – that was a bad mistake. I tried to eat some chocolate but it got blown out of my mouth. I thought 'Shall I go back or go on?'

I managed to keep going because some of the track was in the lee of the ridge. However, around noon I reached a broad ridge with no shelter and I ran out of things to hang on to. I thought perhaps I'd meet someone coming the other way who might help, but I didn't like the look of things. I broke low branches off a big bush and made a wee bivvy and snuggled in there, and just sat till about 5 p.m. with my parka and all my clothes on, and shopping bags wrapped round my legs. I was thinking 'This is pretty dodgy!' The wind was worse but there wasn't much rain, just mist. I could only see about 50 metres. I texted my brother for a weather forecast, but he'd gone out without his cellphone.

By 10 p.m. I was getting a bit cold and less able to think straight. The roaring wind was starting to affect me. Sometimes I thought I heard voices and I was looking around for people. I started to feel weak and vulnerable. I was dehydrated because I hadn't brought much water – but I ate a sandwich.

It was a long night. I dozed a couple of times. I was in a weird space. I'd stopped eating and drinking – I don't know why, perhaps I wanted to conserve what I had. I'd imagined the weather would be better in the morning, but it wasn't. I don't know when the rain started, but I was getting wetter and wetter. I had a strange thing about not wanting to open my pack in case I got my gear wet.

Just after 6.30 a.m. I called 111, but the call-taker was unhelpful so I texted my brother again. He dialled 111 and got an immediate response. I kept thinking I could hear people and I would stand up to look for them; but that only made me wetter and colder. Mentally I said goodbye to my kids and grandkids. I felt I was going to die. There was no way anyone was going to reach me in those conditions.

Around midday there were more voices. I thought, 'I'm sure that's real,' and waved my red bandana. The yelling stopped and I thought, 'Oh my God, they've gone away!' and collapsed in a heap without even covering up.

About a quarter of an hour later I heard the voices again, and this time two people came. They got me into a tent and soon a rescue party arrived. It was 12 or 14 hours before I stopped shivering. We were there for another 48 hours before they carried me down False Spur – I was so weak I could hardly stand – and the helicopter came in. The pilot risked his life to do that. I had nightmares for a fortnight afterwards. The sound of the wind was in my ears for ages.

Johnny Mulheron comments:

- The main contributing factors in this instance were the **misjudging of weather** and **underestimating the physical difficulty** of the tramp.
- Many accidents occur when **desire overrules judgement,** such as pushing on when the prudent decision is to turn back.
- Fatigued **solo trampers** can make less rational decisions without companions to keep them in check.
- In extreme conditions, it becomes absolutely vital to **take shelter** from the conditions and rest, rather than battling on.
- **Inadequate gear** contributed to this predicament. Some form of shelter such as a survival bag, flysheet, tarp or bivvy bag would have improved her situation.
- More and more people are texting for help on cellphones, but this can be unreliable: not only do you not know if the recipient has opened and actioned it, but there can be significant network delays in delivering the message. It is better to **ring and speak to emergency services direct**.

Hypothermia

Cold conditions needn't be a problem in themselves. If you are well prepared and on the move, you should be able to stay comfortably warm. However, if the conditions are particularly cold and wet, or you are simply ill-prepared, cold can be a killer.

Hypothermia (also known as **exposure**) is the term used when the body's core temperature drops below 35°c, a condition which accounts for a large number of emergencies in the New Zealand outdoors. Unfortunately, victims of advanced hypothermia don't realise they are in danger – one of the symptoms is irrational behaviour. It is therefore important to recognise the early signs, both in yourself and others: violent shivering, weariness, loss of coordination, incoherence and muscle stiffness. When severe hypothermia sets in, shivering may stop, and the victim may collapse and lapse into unconsciousness. Beyond this stage lurks death.

If you suspect a member of your party is, or is becoming hypothermic, act immediately:

- **Stop and take shelter** – get out of the wind and rain.
- **Warm the victim up** – put more clothing on them or replace wet clothing with dry; pay close attention to the head. Wrap them up in a sleeping bag or survival bag. Water bottles filled with warm water can be placed inside, or if possible, climb inside the bag with them and share your body heat.
- **Make warm, sweet liquids to drink** – they will help heat up the victim from the inside.
- **Monitor the victim** for changes in temperature and level of consciousness.
- **Do not** rub the victim or give them alcohol as this encourages blood to move to the skin's surface, away from vital organs.

All going well, the victim will appear to recover quickly. However, do not press on too swiftly as they may collapse again. It may take up to two days to fully recover.

> **I REMEMBER HEARING** about exposure after I'd been tramping a few years, and realised that I had had it several times. (No one had noticed though, because I tended to act irrationally, slur my words and stumble at the best of times!)
>
> Graeme Dingle,
> *The Outdoor World of Graeme Dingle*, 1983

HIGH HILLS

Gently let my ashes rest
Mid the high hills of the west,
Where the golden tussocks grow
And the graceful red deer go.

Where down in the gorges dim
Blue ducks of the mountains swim,
And the red stag's roar resound
Through my happy hunting ground.

While through beeches straight and tall
Mountain breezes softly call,
And the mad world's worries cease
Mid those ancient hills of peace.

There forgotten tracks I'll tramp,
Forgotten make the final camp
Where bellbirds sing the best
Mid the high hills of the west.

For remembrance only these,
Lofty hills and stately trees,
Azure lake and rippling shore,
Grace of life for evermore.

Lester Masters, 1958

Glossary

back country 'The land remote from coastal settlements or from settled districts; the hinterland of a settlement or of a port; the parts of a sheep-station remote from the homestead.' (*Oxford Dictionary of New Zealand English*)

bivvy or **bivouac** a rough shelter or sheltered camping place

bluff cliff, or steep hill

bushline line above which native forest stops growing, usually around 1000 to 1500 metres above sea level

cairn a mound of stones signalling a track or change in track direction

crampons spikes strapped to boots for climbing ice and walking on snow

DOC Department of Conservation

ELB emergency locator beacon

freedom camping camping away from designated campsites

gaiter nylon or Gore-Tex covering that extends from the soles on one's boots to just below the knee, designed to prevent debris from entering the boot

giardia a genus of protozoa that may be parasitic in the intestines of vertebrates including humans and most domestic animals

GPS Global Positioning System. Usually in the form of a handheld device that provides your location on the globe in longitude, latitude and elevation

long drop the ubiquitous back-country toilet, consisting of a basic shelter, toilet seat and ... a long drop (hopefully)

MRS Mountain Radio Service

MSC Mountain Safety Council

puttee the ankle-length version of the gaiter

route a feasible passage from A to B but not necessarily marked and often difficult

saddle a low passage over a ridge. Usually the easiest route between two valley systems

scree loose soil or stones

scroggin trail mix

swingbridge suspension bridge usually constructed from wire or rope and wood

switchback zig-zag path up a slope

tarn small mountain pond or lake, often created by glacial movement

three-wire bridge river/stream crossing consisting of three cables, one for the feet and two for hanging onto

trail head start/finish of the track

woop-woops the name applied in jest to small, remote or back-country areas

See page 52 for meteorological (i.e. weather) terms.

An alternative glossary

These entries are just some from a list which first appeared in *Wilderness* magazine ('A New Dictionary of Outdoor Terminology'), reproduced by kind permission of Shaun Barnett and Dave Chowdhury.

bevvy an alcoholic beverage, perhaps port or Stones Green Ginger Wine, consumed with great relish whilst your party of six is crammed into a two-person bivvy during a storm

bowling the billy the act of knocking the billy off the burner and spilling all of the contents on the ground just as the stew has boiled

bully tea brew made with endangered native freshwater fish

bushcline the act of prostrating oneself whilst crawling through subalpine scrub such as leatherwood

cramper person who hogs space in the tent

gored-tex what happens to your $800 jacket after a period of bushclining (see above)

grate walk unpleasant foot abrasion that occurs when the track surface is too hardened

interpretation painel what one experiences when reading too much information about an historic site

long drip a freshly dug long drop hole

loose down sleeping bag an inferior bag in which the down always gathers at the bottom, leaving it with no insulation properties

notional park a good idea for a park

park rager park ranger who goes off at you for not paying your hut fees

pong drop a long drop that needs a freshly dug hole

scraggin when two trampers wrestle over the last of the scroggin

trampler a tramper who tears around the hills at great speed, stomping over rare plants in alpine bogs, and crushing delicate orchids on the forest floor

waking pole device used to rouse snorers from the safety of the far side of the hut

weather vain a guide to looking good for all outdoor occasions

Useful contacts

Department of Conservation Te Papa Atawhai, www.doc.govt.nz
Information on tracks, huts and bookings, intentions lodgements, and much more besides. More than 80 local and area offices and visitor centres around New Zealand.

Department of Conservation Hotline, tel: 0800-362-468
For reporting track hazards such slips, washed out bridges, fires, etc.

Federated Mountain Clubs, www.fmc.org.nz, PO Box 1604, Wellington
The national association of alpine and tramping clubs. They hold details of all local clubs and run training workshops too.

Fish and Game New Zealand, www.fishandgame.co.nz
Fishing and hunting licences.

Forest and Bird, www.forestandbird.org.nz, PO Box 631, Wellington
An independent conservation organisation; particularly good at getting children interested in the outdoors.

MetService, www.metservice.co.nz, tel 0900-999 + your area code
Weather forecasts.

Mountain Radio Service, www.mountainradio.co.nz, tel 03 379-7905
Hires out high-frequency radios and operates nationwide communication centres.

Mountain Safety Council, www.mountainsafety.org.nz, PO Box 6207, Wellington
Promoter of safety in the outdoors. Publishes useful manuals and pamphlets and runs public courses such as first aid and bushcraft.

New Zealand Tramper, www.tramper.co.nz
A useful website with track specifics, online forum and articles.

Visitor Information Network, www.newzealand.com/travel/vins
The national network of visitor centres providing free information and assistance with bookings.

Further reading

Last summer, on a recommendation from a friend, I borrowed from the library *Pioneers of Martins Bay*, Alice McKenzie's memoir of growing up in a wild and remote extremity of Fiordland over 120 years ago. I read it during the four-day tramp down the Hollyford Valley to the sea, where Martins Bay is found, truly isolated, other-worldly and incredibly beautiful. Just to be in that magical place was ample reward for our efforts. But Alice's stories resonated all around, adding so much depth and texture: the epic and sometimes tragic journeys made between Gunn's Camp and Jamestown – the promising settlement that was never delivered, (now but a ghost); the family left half-starving when the four-monthly steamship passed them by; and the ultimate failure of cattle-farming in a place so barely pastoral that even if you kept the beasts alive they'd be lucky to survive the drive to market. And all of this before the invention of insect mesh and Gore-Tex.

Don't Forget Your Scroggin is, we hope, the beginning of a journey that will take you further, deeper (and safely) into that other world. Here's our list of some good books to set you on your way and keep you going – most of which are readily available from bookshops or your local library. And don't forget about *Te Ara*, the excellent online encyclopedia of New Zealand, www.teara.govt.nz.

Guidebooks, maps and atlases

Arthur's Pass to Mount Cook: a tramping guide, Sven Brabyn, Brabyn Publishing, 2004

Canterbury Foothills & Forests: a walking and tramping guide, Pat Barrett, Shoal Bay Press, 2002

Classic Tramping in New Zealand, Shaun Barnett and Rob Brown, Craig Potton Publishing, 1999

Classic Walks of New Zealand, Craig Potton, Craig Potton Publishing, 1997

Bird's Eye Day Walks in New Zealand: 100 great short tracks, Shaun Barnett with maps by Geographx, Craig Potton Publishing, 2007

The Geographic Atlas of New Zealand, Geographx, Craig Potton Publishing, 2005

Moir's Guide North – The Otago Southern Alps, (7th edition), Geoff Spearpoint (ed.), New Zealand Alpine Club, 2005

National Parks and Other Wild Places of New Zealand, Kathy Ombler, New Holland, 2001

North Island Weekend Tramps, Shaun Barnett, Craig Potton Publishing, 2004

South Island Weekend Tramps, Nick Groves, Craig Potton Publishing, 2003

Tararua Footprints: a tramper's guide to the Tararua Ranges, Merv Rodgers, Canterbury University Press, 1996

Bird's Eye Tramping in New Zealand: 40 great New Zealand tramping trips, Shaun Barnett with maps by Geographx, Craig Potton Publishing, 2006

Tramping in the South Island, Mount Richmond Forest Park to Arthur's Pass, Sven Brabyn, Brabyn Publishing, 2003

Westland Foothills & Forests: a walking and tramping guide, Pat Barrett, Shoal Bay, 2004

Natural history and field guides

Bushcraft, New Zealand Mountain Safety Council, 1996

Common Birds in New Zealand and *Rare Birds of New Zealand*, Geoff Moon, Reed, 1995

Collins Birds of New Zealand, Chloë Talbot Kelly, HarperCollins, 2006

Flight of the Huia: ecology and conservation of New Zealand's frogs, reptiles, birds and mammals, Kerry-Jane Wilson, Canterbury University Press, 2004

Ghosts of Gondwana: the history of life in New Zealand, George Gibbs, Craig Potton Publishing, 2006

How to Gaze at the Southern Stars, Richard Hall, Awa Press, 2004

Landforms: the shaping of New Zealand, Les Molly and Roger Smith, Craig Potton Publishing, 2002

Nature Guide to the New Zealand Forest, John Dawson and Rob Lucas, Godwit, 2000

The New Zealand Weather Book, Erick Brenstrum, Craig Potton Publishing, 1998

New Zealand's Wilderness Heritage, Les Molloy and Craig Potton, Craig Potton Publishing, 2007

Photographic Guide to New Zealand Alpine Plants, Lawrie Metcalf, New Holland, 2007

Photographic Guide to New Zealand Insects, Brian Parkinson and Don Horne, New Holland, 2007

Our Islands, Our Selves: a history of conservation in New Zealand, David Young, Otago University Press, 2004

Take A Kid Outdoors, Colin Moore, New Holland, 2006

Where to Watch Birds in New Zealand, Kathy Ombler, New Holland, 2007

History and biography

anything by *Graeme Dingle*

anything by or about *Sir Edmund Hillary*

anything by or about *John Pascoe*

A Trampers Journey, Mark Pickering, Craig Potton Publishing, 2005

Fiordland Explored: an illustrated history, John Hall-Jones, Craig Printing, 1997

The Hills, Mark Pickering, Heinemann Reed, 1988

Mountain Solitudes, Aat Vervoorn, Craig Potton Publishing, 2000

The Nature of Things: poems from the New Zealand landscape, James Brown (ed.) and Craig Potton, Craig Potton Publishing, 2005

Pioneers of Martins Bay: the story of New Zealand's most remote settlement, Alice McKenzie, Lakes District Museum, 2006

Stewart Island Explored, John Hall-Jones, Craig Printing, 1998

Te Araroa: the New Zealand Trail, Geoff Chapple, Random House, 2002

Magazines

Federated Mountain Clubs bulletin (four issues per annum), www.fmc.org.nz

New Zealand Geographic (bi-monthly), www.nzgeographic.co.nz

NZ Wilderness (monthly), www.wildernessmag.com

About the authors

Sarah Bennett grew up in Blenheim. It was a school class tramp in Nelson Lakes National Park that piqued her interest in the outdoors (thanks to teacher Mr David Rees – up to this point unacknowledged). But she didn't really get into tramping with any real vigour until she met Lee, while living in England.

Lee Slater, an Essex lad, was first bitten by the tramping bug in the Highlands of Scotland, the Yorkshire Moors and Peak District of England whilst at college and university.

Lee and Sarah have rambled around Great Britain and hiked 11 national parks in the USA. They have tramped many corners of Aotearoa since their return in 1999, and walk uphill daily to their home on Mount Pleasant, Wellington.

Acknowledgements

First and foremost, a big thank you to everyone we've tramped with and met on the track over the years: almost without exception a lovely bunch of people indeed.

For assistance with the early draft, thanks to Simon and Stephanie Smith. For various services including fact checking, feedback and advice, thanks to Ryan at Macpac; Daniel, Blair and Cliff at Tisdalls (missing you already); the folks at Bivouac; and Rob at Kiwi Outdoors Centre. Thanks also to Richard Saunders and Edwina Clarke, Okarito Nature Tours, for their repellent recipe.

For tips and assistance with content, thanks to DOC – particularly Robert Hawke and Fiona Colquhoun, and Cristina Samson at the Mountain Safety Council. To all those people whom we rang with curly questions to do with obscure statistics, dehydrators, etc., and those people whose ears we bent about noodles, thanks to you too.

Numerous people have been quoted in these pages – thanks for sharing your stories. Particular thanks to Polly Greeks, Kelvin Lloyd, Mark Pickering, Johnny Mulheron and anonymous survivor. To those who remain undesirably anonymous, we'd love you to step forward and identify yourselves.

Shaun Barnett gets special mention: he has been enormously helpful in the latter stages of writing this book and actually deserves a medal (so we're having one forged as we write). You're an absolute winner.

We would like to hereby acknowledge the people at Craig Potton Publishing. You do our country a great service by continuing to publish books that encourage us to enjoy and cherish our great outdoors. Special thanks to Gwen Redshaw, who came up with the concept and title for this book, and to Robbie, Betzy and Phillippa: your encouragement is much appreciated.

Finally, a big thank you from Sarah to Lee: thanks for making all our tramping trips so much fun.

Trip planning checklist

- ☐ map and/or route guide
- ☐ transport
- ☐ clothing
- ☐ equipment
- ☐ food and water
- ☐ bookings
- ☐ weather forecast
- ☐ track conditions ascertained
- ☐ intentions lodged
- ☐ Plan B (i.e. alternative route) and emergency plan

Equipment checklist

Essentials for overnight trips [Items in brackets may not be necessary]

- [ ] pack and waterproof liner
- [ ] map(s) [compass]
- [ ] food and water
- [ ] first aid kit
- [ ] tent and repair kit
- [ ] sunblock and insect repellent
- [ ] toilet gear and pack towel
- [ ] toilet paper [trowel]
- [ ] assorted spare plastic bags
- [ ] hut tickets (or money for hut fees)
- [ ] cooking stove and fuel
- [ ] sleeping bag [liner and sleeping mat]
- [ ] cooking and eating utensils, pocket knife
- [ ] torch with spare bulb and batteries [lantern and fuel]
- [ ] clothing for all weathers
- [ ] water bottles [filter/purification]
- [ ] survival bag/emergency blanket and whistle
- [ ] dishwashing liquid and scourer [laundry soap and elastic washing line]

Optional extras

- [ ] sunglasses
- [ ] camera
- [ ] binoculars
- [ ] field guides
- [ ] watch
- [ ] candles
- [ ] pen or pencil and paper
- [ ] fire starters
- [ ] walking stick
- [ ] deck of cards or other small games, hacky sack, frisbee
- [ ] mobile telephone, mountain radio, GPS or locator beacon

Clothing and footwear checklist

Summer day trips

- ☐ sun hat
- ☐ raincoat
- ☐ medium weight top
- ☐ thick socks and boots
- ☐ heavier weight jumper, fleece or soft-shell
- ☐ t-shirt or long-sleeve breathable top
- ☐ shorts or lightweight zip-off pants
- ☐ bandana
- ☐ warm hat, if it could turn cold

Remember: even on a glorious summer day, the weather can change quickly – especially in alpine environments. Always be prepared for the worst conditions: you may need extra warm layers or waterproofs.

All other trips

- ☐ sun hat and warm hat
- ☐ medium weight top
- ☐ thick socks and boots
- ☐ puttees or gaiters
- ☐ lightweight hut shoes
- ☐ longjohns
- ☐ shorts or trousers
- ☐ waterproof overtrousers
- ☐ raincoat
- ☐ gloves or mittens
- ☐ wool or polypropylene undergarments
- ☐ heavier weight jumper, fleece or soft-shell

Index